"From the first page, the reader of *How to Read a Poem* realises that this, at last, is a book which begins to answer Adrian Mitchell's charge: 'Most people ignore most poetry because most poetry ignores most people'. Eagleton introduces himself as 'a politically minded literary theorist'. The remarkable achievement of this book is to prove that such a theorist is the only person who can really show what poetry is for. By a brilliant and scrupulous series of readings – of Yeats and Frost and Auden and Dickinson – framed in a lively account of the function of criticism as perhaps only he could expound it, Eagleton shows how literary theory, seriously understood, is the ground of poetic understanding. This will be the indispensable apology for poetry in our time."

Bernard O'Donoghue, Wadham College, University of Oxford

Terry Eagleton

The author is John Edward Taylor Professor of English Literature at the University of Manchester. His recent publications include *The English Novel* (2004), *Sweet Violence: The Idea of the Tragic* (2003), *The Idea of Culture* (2000), *Scholars and Rebels in Nineteenth-Century Ireland* (1999), *Literary Theory: An Introduction* (second edition, 1996) and *The Illusions of Postmodernism* (1996), all published by Blackwell Publishing.

Contents

Preface

This book is designed as an introduction to poetry for students and general readers. I have tried to make what some find an intimidating subject as lucid and accessible as possible; but some bits of the book are inevitably harder going than others. Less experienced readers might therefore prefer to start with Chapter 4 ('In Pursuit of Form'), Chapter 5 ('How To Read A Poem') and Chapter 6 ('Four Nature Poems'), before moving on to the more theoretical chapters. Even so, I think the book makes more sense if it is read from start to finish.

I am deeply grateful to John Barrell at York University, Stan Smith at Nottingham Trent University, Emma Bennett, Philip Carpenter and Astrid Wind at Blackwell, and William Flesch at Brandeis University for their helpful suggestions.

TE
Dublin, 2005

Chapter 1

The Functions of Criticism

1.1   The End of Criticism?

I first thought of writing this book when I realised that hardly any of the students of literature I encountered these days practised what I myself had been trained to regard as literary criticism. Like thatching or clog dancing, literary criticism seems to be something of a dying art. Since many of these students are bright and capable enough, the fault would seem to lie largely with their teachers. The truth is that quite a few teachers of literature nowadays do not practise literary criticism either, since they, in turn, were never taught to do so.

This charge may seem pretty rich, coming as it does from a literary theorist. Wasn't it literary theory, with its soulless abstractions and vacuous generalities, which destroyed the habit of close reading in the first place? I have pointed out elsewhere that this is one of the great myths or unexamined clichés of contemporary critical debate.[1] It is one of those 'everybody knows' pieties, like the assumption that serial killers look just like you and me, keep themselves to themselves, but always have a polite word for their neighbours. It is as much a shop-soiled banality as the claim that Christmas has become dreadfully commercialised. Like all tenacious myths which refuse to vanish whatever the evidence, it is there to serve specific interests. The idea that literary theorists killed poetry dead because with their shrivelled hearts and swollen brains they are incapable of spotting a metaphor, let alone a

---

[1]   See, among other places, Terry Eagleton, *After Theory* (London, 2003), p. 93.

1

tender feeling, is one of the more obtuse critical platitudes of our time. The truth is that almost all major literary theorists engage in scrupulously close reading. The Russian Formalists on Gogol or Pushkin, Bakhtin on Rabelais, Adorno on Brecht, Benjamin on Baudelaire, Derrida on Rousseau, Genette or de Man on Proust, Hartman on Wordsworth, Kristeva on Mallarmé, Jameson on Conrad, Barthes on Balzac, Iser on Henry Fielding, Cixous on Joyce, Hillis Miller on Henry James, are just a handful of examples.

Some of these figures are not only eminent critics, but literary artists in their own right. They produce literature in the act of commenting on it. Michel Foucault is another such outstanding stylist. It is true that thinkers like these have sometimes been ill served by their disciples, but the same goes for some non-theoretical critics. But the point, in any case, is irrelevant. For it is not as though many students of literature today do not read poems and novels fairly closely. Close reading is not the issue. The question is not how tenaciously you cling to the text, but what you are in search of when you do so. The theorists I have mentioned are not only close readers, but are sensitive to questions of literary form. And this is where they differ from most students today.

It is significant, in fact, that if you broach the question of form with students of literature, some of them think that you are talking simply about metre. 'Paying attention to form', in their eyes, means saying whether the poem is written in iambic pentameters, or whether it rhymes. Literary form obviously includes such things; but saying what the poem means, and then tagging on a couple of sentences about its metre or rhyme scheme, is not exactly engaging with questions of form. Most students, faced with a novel or poem, spontaneously come up with what is commonly known as 'content analysis'. They give accounts of works of literature which describe what is going on in them, perhaps with a few evaluative comments thrown in. To adopt a technical distinction from linguistics, they treat the poem as *language* but not as *discourse*.

'Discourse', as we shall see, means attending to language in all of its material density, whereas most approaches to poetic language tend to disembody it. Nobody has ever heard language pure and simple. Instead, we hear utterances that are shrill or sardonic, mournful or nonchalant, mawkish or truculent, irascible or histrionic. And this, as we shall see, is part of what we mean by form. People sometimes talk about digging out the ideas 'behind' the poem's language, but this spatial metaphor is misleading. For it is not as though the language is a kind of disposable cellophane in which the ideas come ready-wrapped. On the contrary, the language of a poem is *constitutive* of its ideas.

anthropology, but you cannot make a scientific study of the retired admiral in the cottage down the road.

So the prejudice that poetry deals above all in concrete particulars is actually fairly recent. In one sense, to be sure, it runs back all the way to Plato, who saw poetry as an ungovernable mob of unruly particulars, and banished it from his ideal state for much the same reasons that he expelled democracy. Aristotle, by contrast, saw poetry as dealing in universals; while for some early Christian thinkers like St Augustine, to attend to the particular as an end in itself, rather than to read it 'semiotically' as a sign of God's presence in the world, was an act of impiety. It is really with the growth of modern aesthetics in the mid-eighteenth century, and then with the flourishing of Romanticism, that the idea of concrete particularity as precious in itself burst upon the literary scene in a big way. The assumption that poetry busies itself with the sensuously specific, and is sceptical of general ideas, would no doubt have come as a mighty surprise to Aristotle, Dante, Shakespeare, Milton, Pope and Johnson. It would even have been news to a good many Romantics. There is hardly much sensuous specificity in Wordsworth. Not all poets have subscribed to the dangerous doctrine that only what we feel on the pulses is true. It is a belief at least as typical of neo-fascists as it is of creative artists. A nervousness of general ideas is as much a mark of the philistine as the poet.

In any case, if some Romantics insisted on the sensuous particularity of the poem, they were also inclined to speak of its universal nature. And the two would seem hard to reconcile. Even so, a resolution lay conveniently to hand, known as the symbol. The Romantic symbol is supposed to flesh out a universal truth in a uniquely specific form. In some mysterious fashion it combines the individual and the universal, setting up a direct circuit between the two which bypasses language, history, culture and rationality. To penetrate to the essence of what makes a thing uniquely itself is to discover the part it plays in the cosmic whole. This idea runs steadily through Western civilisation, all the way from Plato's Forms and Leibniz's monads to Hegel's World Spirit, Coleridge's symbols and Hopkins's 'inscapes'. What it meant in the case of poetry, translated into rather less exalted terms, was that poets now had two ways at their disposal of avoiding actual history. They could look 'below' it, to the ineffably particular; or they could rise above it to universal truths. With the aid of the symbol, they could even do both at the same time.

In going transcendent, poetry in the Romantic period cut increasingly adrift from the public world, moving both upward and inward. Yet it was also its very distance from that public sphere which allowed it to act as a critique of it, and so to engage with it after a fashion. The imagination soared higher than prosaic reality, but in poets like Blake and Shelley it still figured as a transformative political force. It could conjure up enthralling new possibilities of social existence; or it could insist upon the contrast between its own sublime energies and a drably mechanistic social order. Poetry could model a type of human creativity, along with 'organic' rather than instrumental relationships, which were less and less to be found in industrial society as a whole.

In Victorian England, this sense of the imagination as a political force gradually faded. It was still eloquently at work in the writings of John Ruskin and William Morris; but poetry, according to John Stuart Mill, was now to be overheard rather than heard. It had retreated from the public forum to the parlour. Having begun life as a sub-branch of rhetoric, it was now the precise opposite of it. Despite the enormous public esteem bestowed on the most eminent poets of the age, poetry itself had essentially been privatised. Tennyson might hold the public post of Poet Laureate, but his finest writing was more lyrical than epic, more tremulously introspective than robustly *engagé*. Challenged by the most powerful public genre of the age (the novel), and spurned by the dominant philosophy of Utilitarianism, poetry was in danger of being overlooked rather than overheard. In a new division of literary labour, the novel was now seen as a social form, dealing in ideas and institutions, while poetry had become the preserve of personal feeling. It was as though the lyric poem defined the entire genre. So it would remain, until modernists like Eliot, Yeats, Pound and Stevens sought to revive it as a major genre. Perhaps poetry might become a central art form once again in a modern age whose sense of solitude and spiritual anxiety matched its own. Perhaps it was in articulating this intensely private experience that it could, ironically, become most publicly representative.

The story of rhetoric, then, is not an encouraging one. After a promising start in the ancient city-states, it was fossilised by the medieval scholars, suppressed by scientific rationalism, and finally routed by a privatised poetics. A sophisticated ancient art ended up as synonymous with tub-thumping, brazen cajolery and the cynical inciting of mass emotion. In the United States today, it means teaching freshmen where to insert semicolons. The art of rhetoric did, however, exact a belated sort of revenge. In his notes on the subject, Friedrich Nietzsche argues that the study of rhetoric as the art of public persuasion should play second fiddle to the study of it as a set of tropes and figures – figures, he comments, which are the 'truest nature' of language as such. What Nietzsche did was to generalise rhetoric (in the sense of figurative or non-literal discourse) to the whole of our speech. All language worked by metaphor, metonymy, synecdoche, chiasmus and the like; and this

the poet either. You could write in a private language known only to your-self; but to code and decode your experience in this way, indeed to have the concepts of 'code' and 'decode' in the first place, you would already need a language learned from and shared with others, who could therefore in prin-ciple come to decipher what you had written.

Many poems do not actually have an original context, since the experiences they portray are purely imaginary. There was no real situation in the first place. We have no idea whether Shakespeare ever called down frightful curses upon his treacherous daughters while crazed and naked on a heath, and from a critical viewpoint it does not matter whether he did or not. It is not the experience 'behind' *Lear* which concerns us, but the experience which *is* the play. T. S. Eliot once remarked that a genuine poet was one who wrote about experiences before they had happened to him.[2] In any case, not all poems register 'experiences'; what 'experience' does Homer's *Iliad* or Alexander Pope's *Essay on Criticism* reflect?

Even so, this is not quite what we mean by calling these works fictional. 'Fictional' does not primarily mean 'imaginary'. As far as fictionalising goes, it does not really matter whether the experience in question actually happened or not. Even if we discovered that there was a real-life Victorian orphan called Oliver Twist, it would make no difference to our 'uptake' of the work in which he appears. Some of the experiences recorded in Charlotte Brontë's novels actually happened to her, and some did not; but we do not need to know which is which in order to respond to her writing. An historically challenged reader could enjoy *War and Peace* without knowing that Napoleon actually existed.

If 'fiction' and 'imaginary' are not the same thing, it is partly because not all imaginary experiences are fiction (hallucinations, for example), but also because you can 'fictionalise' a piece of writing which was originally intended as factual. Notes to the milkman are usually terse, to the point, and written in plain, economical style; but this would not prevent a poetically inclined milkman from noting that 'Two skimmed, two semi-skimmed and one full cream' is an iambic pentameter. The meaning of a statement is partly determined by what sort of reception it anticipates; but this does not guar-antee that it will get that sort of reception. We can read fictions non-fictionally, as when I am convinced that *Crime and Punishment* is a secret message about the unhealthy state of my feet addressed to me alone. Or we can read fac-tual discourse fictionally, as when we read a meteorological report so as to

---

[2] Quoted in John Haffenden, *William Empson: Vol. 1: Among the Mandarins* (Oxford, 2005), p. 112.

stimulate in ourselves a sublime sense of the vastness of the skies and the mighty powers of Nature.

A different kind of example can be found in Alan Brownjohn's poem 'Common Sense':

> An agricultural labourer, who has
> A wife and four children, receives 20s a week.
> $^3/_4$ buys food, and the members of the family
> Have three meals a day.
> How much is that per person per meal?
> *–From Pitman's Common Sense Arithmetic, 1917*

> A gardener, paid 24s a week, is
> Fined $^1/_3$ if he comes to work late.
> At the end of 26 weeks, he receives
> £30.5.3. How
> Often was he late?
> *–From Pitman's Common Sense Arithmetic, 1917*

> . . . The table printed below gives the number
> Of paupers in the United Kingdom, and
> The total cost of poor relief.
> Find the average number
> Of paupers per ten thousand people.
> *–From Pitman's Common Sense Arithmetic, 1917*

> . . . Out of an army of 28,000 men,
> 15% were
> Killed, 25% were
> Wounded. Calculate
> How many men were there left to fight?
> *–From Pitman's Common Sense Arithmetic, 1917*

The poem is presumably not primarily aimed at those with an interest in the history of arithmetical textbooks. Instead, it sheds some light on what counts at various times as common sense, which is a moral rather than empirical matter, and thus the kind of stuff in which poems trade. The supposedly most dispassionate of human languages – mathematics – is revealed to be interwoven with ideological assumptions. Why should one take it for granted, for example, that those left alive should carry on fighting? Why not surrender? By breaking lines from the textbook up on the page, Brownjohn can turn them into a moral statement without altering a word. Pitman's phrases have now been reoriented. They have accrued a different sort of meaning from the one they would have for a school pupil in the First World War trying to solve these sums.

Fiction, then, does not mean in the first place 'factually false'. There are lots of falsehoods which are not fictional, and, as we have seen, there are also lots of factually true statements in literary works. The word 'fiction' is a set of rules for how we are to *apply* certain pieces of writing – rather as the rules of chess tell us not whether the chess pieces are solid or hollow, but how we are to move them around. Fiction instructs us in what we are to do with texts, not in how true or false they are. It suggests, for example, that we should not take them primarily as factual propositions, or worry overmuch about whether what factual claims they do contain are true or false. These claims, fiction informs us, are there mostly in the service of moral truth; they are not present for their own sake.

Fiction, then, is the kind of place in which the moral holds sway over the empirical – in which what holds our attention is, say, the significance of Fagin's matted red hair, not how many red-haired Jewish child-corrupters there actually were in Victorian London. This is not to dismiss such questions as pointless: it says quite a bit about Dickens that he should make one of the only two Jewish characters in his novels a villain. (The other was portrayed favourably in a feeble attempt to compensate for the first.) The way literary works rig the empirical evidence may be part of their moral meaning. And you cannot identify this rigging without empirical research.

Even so, if we read *Oliver Twist* for historical information about Victorian workhouses, we are not reading the novel as fiction – even though everything in it, including the information it provides about Victorian workhouses, *is* fiction. This information is fictional, as we have seen already, because it is there not for its own sake but as part of an overall rhetorical design. It is there to help construct what we might call a moral vision or way of seeing; and it is certainly possible for us to say whether we think *this* is true or false, feeble or powerful, frivolous or illuminating. But moral visions are not true or false in the same way that statements of fact are.

The fact that what is mainly at stake in literature are moral rather than empirical claims means that writers can bend the latter to fit the former. Aristotle remarks that the poet, unlike the historian, does not have to stick to the way things are. Because literary works, including historical novels, are not obliged to conform closely to the historical facts, they can reorganise those facts so as to highlight their moral significance. Narratives usually reconfigure the world in order to make a point about it. If you are writing a novel about Byron, you might feel it more appropriate to have him die fighting in the struggle for Greek national independence rather than unheroically succumbing to a fever in the midst of it, which was how he actually met his end. It might even seem more 'true'. History does not always get the facts in the most satisfactory order, or stage its events in the most convincing way. It was an absurd oversight on history's part to make Napoleon so stunted, or to cram so many wars into the twentieth century rather than spacing them out a bit more.

If we do not treat *Oliver Twist* 'fictionally', there is a danger that we will read it as just another real-life biography, and so fail to grasp its deeper implications. Its moral impact might be muffled if we take it too literally. Yet for the work to make such an impact, it needs to have an air of reality about it. The more realist it is, the more its moral significance is intensified; but for just the same reason, the more it is endangered. The ambiguous message of a work of literature, then, is 'Take me as real, but don't take me as real.' In one sense, poems, particularly post-Romantic ones, can seem *more* real, in the sense of more vitally present, more sensuously specific and emotionally intense, than the tarnished, abstraction-ridden everyday world. In another sense, as we have seen, they are less real, in the sense of less empirical, than most other forms of writing.

Just as there are risks in reading poems too literally, so there are dangers in generalising their meaning too far. We might come to believe, disastrously, that all the moral truths we encounter in literature are universally valid ones. We might read *Oliver Twist* not as portraying a situation which is in some sense remediable, but as an unalterable part of the human condition. We would thus find ourselves taking the view of the Victorian Poor Law Commissioners, who held for the most part that poverty was divinely ordained. This would be particularly ironic, since some of the social abuses which Dickens's novel depicts had in fact disappeared by the time it was published.

To generalise the meaning of a poem does not mean to treat the poem as an allegory of universal truth. On the contrary, part of the point of Romantic and post-Romantic poetry, as we have seen already, is to restore a sense of specificity in an increasingly abstract society. It is something like this, perhaps, which the delicate poem 'Sea Violet' by H. D. (Hilda Doolittle) intends to do:

> The white violet
> is scented on its stalk,
> the sea-violet
> fragile as agate,
> lies fronting all the wind
> among the torn shells
> on the sand-bank.

> The greater blue violets
> flutter on the hill,
> but who would change for these
> who would change for these
> one root of the white sort?
>
> Violet
> your grasp is frail
> on the edge of the sand-hill,
> but you catch the light –
> frost, a star edges with its fire.

The violet is not particularly meant to be 'symbolic'. But this does not mean that the poem is simply a description of an individual flower, without deeper, more complex resonances. Indeed, one of those resonances lies in the very sensuous detail of the piece – in the unwaveringly focused attention it trains upon this fragile, vulnerable form of life. It is this tender sensitivity to the particular, if you like, which is part of its more general significance.

One might say the same of some of John Clare's Nature poetry:

> When midnight comes a host of dogs and men
> Go out and track the badger to his den,
> And put a sack within the hole, and lie
> Till the old grunting badger passes by.
> He comes and hears – they let the strongest loose.
> The old fox hears the noise and drops the goose.
> The poacher shoots and hurries from the cry,
> And the old hare half wounded buzzes by.
> They get a forked stick to bear him down
> And clap the dogs and take him to the town,
> And bait him all the day with many dogs,
> And laugh and shout and fright the scampering hogs.
> He runs along and bites at all he meets:
> They shout and hollo down the noisy streets.
>
> ('Badger')

The strength of these jagged, busily energetic lines lies not just in the way they casually turn their back on verbal adornment, but also in the way they resist any attempt to 'symbolise' the experience in question, making it speak portentously of more than itself. Clare's language is sinewy rather than suggestive. Both aspects of the piece are all the more effective for being quite unselfconscious. There is no programmatic, *Lyrical Ballads*-like attempt at 'plain language' here, simply a taken-for-granted trust in the robustness and resilience of common speech. 'Buzzes' is an especially fine stroke, one which (like 'old' fox and 'old' hare) captures less a quality of the animal itself than the poet's sense of affectionate familiarity with it.

Here as elsewhere, Clare stitches some of his lines together with a simple, repetitive copula ('And') – a device you can also find, though much more cultically and self-consciously, in a good deal of post-Hemingway American prose. He avoids stately or convoluted syntax for a sense of headlong narrative excitement. Unlike more 'polite' eighteenth-century poets, for example, he tends to steer well clear of sub-clauses. There is very little grammatical subordination of one thing to another, or sense of foreground and background. Instead, everything seems to exist on the same level, without proportion or perspective. The verse is written in a rapid, tumbling sort of iambic pentameter: we take in a line, but as we do so look expectantly to what's round the next line-ending.

The structure of the poem is metonymic (a matter of linking items together) rather than metaphorical (grasping affinities between them). There is no apparent concern for overall structure. Things sit haphazardly side by side simply because that is the way they occur in real life. Apart from a general air of fun and riot, one perhaps a little offensive to our more ecologically sensitive ears, the verse seems to feel no need to imply any complex attitude to what it records. Instead, its language effaces itself before what it registers. Its present tense catches the turmoil of the hunt as it happens, but it is also a timeless present which suggests that the badger-baiting has a venerable tradition behind it. So our sense of dramatic high jinks is blended with a bolstering sense of custom and stability.

2.4 Poetry and Pragmatism

Another way of putting the point about fiction is to claim that poems invite us to treat what they say 'non-pragmatically'. They are not about getting something done in a practical, immediate sense, even if they may get things done in some more indirect sense. The British national anthem 'God Save The Queen' is a kind of prayer – one which, like any petitionary prayer, expresses a hope that God will be gracious enough to do what we ask (namely, save the monarch) as a direct result of our mouthing the words. But the speech act is really non-pragmatic: it gives voice to this hope in order to express one's reverence for the head of state. Most British people who sing the national anthem are not cast into suicidal disillusion when, having lustily bellowed out these lines, they discover that the Queen remains as stubbornly unsaved as ever, every bit as stingy to her servants as she was when they started.

We could imagine the legendary anthropologist from Alpha Centauri listening to our speech and not realising that it was meant, among other things, to get things done – not grasping the connections between what we said and what we did, or even that such connections existed. In a sense, he would be hearing our language as poetry – as a verbal ceremony which existed for its own sake. Yet this ceremony itself is part of what we do, and has practical consequences for the rest of our way of life. Poetry is a social institution. It has complex affinities with other parts of our cultural existence. Treating language as not directly related to a material situation, for example, demands a great deal of material stage-setting.

The idea of poetry as a non-pragmatic discourse might be illuminated by this William Carlos Williams poem, which reads like a message to his wife:

> This is Just to Say
>
> I have eaten
> the plums
> that were in
> the icebox
>
> and which
> you were probably
> saving
> for breakfast
>
> Forgive me
> they were delicious
> so sweet
> and so cold

The poem might even have *been* a message to his wife. There is a parody of the piece by Kenneth Koch:

> I chopped down the house that you had been saving to live in next summer.
> I am sorry, but it was morning, and I had nothing to do
> and its wooden beams were so inviting.
>
> We laughed at the hollyhocks together
> and then I sprayed them with lye.
> Forgive me, I simply do not know what I am doing.

I gave away the money that you had been saving to live on for the next
    ten years.
The man who asked for it was shabby
and the firm March wind on the porch was so juicy and cold.

Last evening we were dancing and I broke your leg.
Forgive me. I was clumsy, and
I wanted you here in the wards, where I am a doctor!

(Williams was a physician as well as a poet.) That final exclamation mark is
superfluous, but Koch's parody, as well as being mildly funny, makes an interesting implicit comment on the Williams original. It seems (or pretends) to
see Williams's poem as seeking to excuse selfish and irresponsible behaviour
by appealing to the privileges bestowed on him by the status of poet. Poets,
so the implication runs, believe themselves absolved from common moral
strictures. Their self-centred cult of feeling elevates their own needs over
the claims of others, and the naivety with which they acknowledge this is
simply part of their moral immaturity. Their much-vaunted sensitivity is thus
a kind of callousness.

Perhaps poets can acknowledge their faults as readily as they do because they
know that, like overindulged children, they will be forgiven. The exquisite
sensibility they pride themselves on is really just a form of moral regressive-
ness. In any case, Williams's apology for eating the plums is oddly incoher-
ent: he asks to be forgiven for the act of raiding the plums, appealing to the
fact that they turned out to be delicious. But he could not have known
this when he decided to eat them. What if they had not turned out to be
delicious? It is rather like saying: 'Forgive me for shooting your dog; I got such
a kick out of it.'

There is, however, another way of looking at the piece. This is to see it
less as a poem about the infantile egoism of poets than one about the nature
of poetry itself. The poem is cast in the form of a message, which is a pragmatic piece of language; and it concerns the equally pragmatic or instrumental
action of storing some fruit away in the fridge to eat for breakfast. Putting
the message in this chopped-up form, however, overrides its pragmatic function, rather as the speaker has overridden the pragmatic function of keeping
the fruit for later. What attracted him was the sensuous reality of the plums
themselves, their delectable coldness and sweetness. And this means that
his relation to the plums is more 'poetic' than instrumental. It might be objected
that eating something is quite as pragmatic an activity as putting it in the
icebox; but the point is that the poet 'uses' the plums with full attention to

their specific properties, rather than simply grabbing them as if any old food will do. It is this which forms the basis of his apology, not the more predictable excuse that he was hungry. In fact, he may well not have been; the poem does not propose this at all as a way of exonerating his behaviour.

One thing the poem does, then, apart from fostering in us scriptural reflections about the guilt of eating forbidden fruit, is to show us that the pragmatic and the poetic are not always mutually exclusive. This is also true, as it happens, of Karl Marx's concept of use-value, which involves using things in ways appropriate to their inherent properties. For Marx, the opposite of 'exchange-value', which means a purely instrumental use of objects without regard to their particular features, is not refraining from using things at all, but using them with an eye to their sensuous qualities. So the idea of use-value is an alternative to the aesthete on the one hand, for whom all use is a desecration, and the philistine on the other, who has no feeling for the inner life of things.

In so far as poems, like plums, yield us pleasure, they have a kind of pragmatic function. It is just that this function is closely bound up with their sensuous existence. We do not just use poems instrumentally, any more than the speaker is interested in the plums simply because he is hungry. And just as his relation to the plums is both poetic and pragmatic, so is the text itself, which has the form of a scribbled communication yet which in its last four lines touches on a deeper sort of intensity. 'Forgive me', for example, seems a little histrionic, when 'Sorry' might have done just as well. There is indeed guilt as well as gratification involved in being a poet: it means not relating to the world quite as others do, though this (contrary to popular mythology) springs from being more thoroughly attuned to it, not less. Koch, then, is perhaps not entirely mistaken: a poet can give us a sense of the coldness and sweetness of things, where we might simply see tomorrow morning's breakfast; but to do so involves a 'de-pragmatising' of the world which has its perils as well as its value. One would not usually assign the chair of the famine relief committee to a poet.

2.5   Poetic Language

The final part of our definition to consider is 'verbally inventive'. The phrase is a lame one, but it is probably more accurate than less feeble formulations such as 'verbally self-conscious'. Poetry is often characterised as language which draws attention to itself, or which is focused upon itself, or (as the semiotic jargon has it) language in which the signifier predominates over the signified.

On this theory, poetry is writing which flaunts its material being, rather than modestly effacing it before the Holy-of-Holies of meaning. It is heightened, enriched, intensified speech.

The only problem with this theory is that quite a lot of what we call poetry seems not to behave this way. Take, for example, this passage from Robert Lowell's 'My Last Afternoon with Uncle Devereux Winslow':

> My Uncle was dying at twenty-nine.
> 'You are behaving like children',
> said my Grandfather,
> when my Uncle and Aunt left their three baby daughters,
> and sailed for Europe on a last honeymoon . . .
> I cowered in terror.
> I wasn't a child at all –
> unseen and unseeing. I was Agrippina
> In the Golden House of Nero . . .
> Near me was the white measuring-door
> my Grandfather had pencilled with my Uncle's heights.
> In 1911, he had stopped growing at just six feet . . .

One could imagine this passage written out as prose without it sounding particularly odd, were it not for the suggestive elliptical leaps of lines like 'I cowered in terror. / I wasn't a child at all – unseen and unseeing. / I was Agrippina / In the Golden House of Nero . . .'. Poetry allows for these quick shifts of imaginative logic, in which language works more by compression and association than by fully spelt-out connections. But the first five and last three lines could well appear in the form of prose.

Or take these lines from Ezra Pound's *Cantos*:

> And he came in and said: 'Can't do it,
> Not at that price, we can't do it'.
> That was in the last war, here in England,
> And he was making chunks for a turbine
> In some sort of an army plane;
> An' the inspector says: 'How many rejects?'
> And Joe said: 'We don't get *any* rejects, our . . .'
> And the inspector says: 'Well then of course
> you can't do it'.

It seems stretching a point to see this kind of thing as involving a peculiar verbal self-consciousness, of the kind that one could find, for example, almost anywhere in Gerard Manley Hopkins:

> I caught this morning morning's minion, king-
> dom of daylight's dauphin, dapple-dawn-drawn Falcon, in his riding
> Of the rolling level underneath him steady air, and striding
> High there, how he rung upon the rein of a wimpling wind
> In his ecstasy! . . .
>
> ('The Windhover')

This, admittedly, is a pretty exotic example of the play of the signifier – of language focused flamboyantly upon itself. It is the kind of thing one also finds in certain uses of metre:

> Mine eyes have seen the glory of the coming of the Lord:
> He is trampling out the vintage where the grapes of wrath are stored . . .
>
> (Julia Ward Howe, 'Battle-Hymn of the Republic')

> . . . While I nodded, nearly napping, suddenly there came a tapping,
> As of someone gently rapping, rapping at my chamber door.
> ''Tis some visitor', I murmured, 'tapping at my chamber door –
> Only this and nothing more'.
>
> (Edgar Allan Poe, 'The Raven')

> I went into a public-'ouse to get a pint o'beer,
> The publican 'e up an' sez, 'We serve no red-coats here'.
> The girls be'ind the bar they laughed and giggled fit to die,
> I outs into the street again an' to myself sez I:
> O it's Tommy this, an' Tommy that, an' 'Tommy, go away';
> But it's 'Thank you, Mister Atkins', when the band begins to play . . .
>
> (Rudyard Kipling, 'Tommy')

> By the shores of Gitche Gumee,
> By the shining Big-Sea-Water,
> Stood the wigwam of Nokomis,
> Daughter of the Moon, Nokomis . . .
>
> (Henry Wadsworth Longfellow, 'The Song of Hiawatha')

Metres like these make a terrible racket, making it hard to hear the meaning through their incessant noise. They make the poems seem as though they are really about themselves. Pressed to an extreme, this kind of thing becomes doggerel.

The modern idea of the 'materiality of the signifier' – that the word has its own texture, pitch and density, which poetry exploits more fully than other verbal arts – is probably best exemplified in English not by a modern poet, but by John Milton:

> . . . There was a place
> (Now not, though Sin, not Time, first wrought the change)
> Where Tigris, at the foot of Paradise,
> Into a gulf shot underground, till part
> Rose up a fountain by the Tree of Life.
> In with the river sunk and with it rose
> Satan, involved in rising mist; then sought
> Where to lie hid. Sea he had searched and land,
> From Eden over Pontus, and the pool
> Maeotis, up beyond the river Orb;
> Downward as far antarctic; and, in length,
> West from Orontes to the ocean barred
> At Darien, thence to the land where flows
> Ganges and Indus . . .
>
> (*Paradise Lost*, Book 9)

Reading lines like this is almost a physical labour, as the eye struggles to unravel the intricate syntax and negotiate a path through the bristling thicket of proper names. All the way from that 'Satan' bursting dramatically upon us as we step across from line 6 to line 7, we need to keep the sense of the lines steadily in our heads as we pursue its twists and turns through Milton's grammatical maze. The blank verse slows us down, forcing us to experience the celebrated Miltonic music in all its high-pitched rhetorical bravura. From 'Sea he had searched and land' to 'Ganges and Indus', we seem to be re-enacting Satan's wanderings in the restless shifts and turns of the syntax and laborious pile-up of clauses, no sooner sent off in one fruitless direction than reoriented to another. There is a complex interplay between metre and speaking voice, as each weaves its way in and out of the other. The speaking voice plays across the metrical scheme with the kind of extreme flexibility and variation typical of English blank verse; but the elevated tone of the piece loftily survives all these resourceful syntactical twists and turns.

Poets, then, are materialists of language. Even so, much poetry cultivates the virtues of plainness and transparency. This is particularly true of some eighteenth-century English verse, which displays the Enlightenment virtues of clarity, equipoise and exactness; but it is also true for quite different reasons of a good deal of modern and postmodern poetry. Modernism, among other things, reflects a crisis of faith in language. There is a scepticism of the extravagant metaphor and the histrionic verbal gesture in an age which has good reason to be suspicious of manipulative rhetoric, whether it stems from autocrats or advertisers. There is also a distrust of language in an age when experience seems either too intricate or too appalling to find

The Formalists did not claim that this foregrounding of the sign was confined to literature. 'Literariness' is not the same as 'literature'. Literariness can crop up in jokes or riddles or advertising slogans, while in some works of literature (realist novels, for example) it is fairly rare. Some tabloid newspapers, their editor would be astonished to hear, go in for literariness far more than does George Orwell. 'Making language strange' meant deviating from a linguistic norm, and in doing so 'defamiliarising' our shopsoiled, 'automated' everyday discourse. As such, poetry is a kind of creative deformation of our practical communication. Phrases like 'Thou still unravished bride of quietness' wreak systematic violence on our ordinary speech.

It follows from this that literariness is a relative concept, since you can only spot a deviation if you can identify a norm. And linguistic norms shift around. 'Estrangement' only works against a taken-for-granted linguistic background, but one person's taken-for-granted background may be another person's estrangement. Dropping your aitches in Knightsbridge probably counts as a deviation, whereas it is normative in parts of Lancashire. Pronouncing 'aitch' as 'haitch' is normative in the Republic of Ireland but deviant in Devon. To pronounce 'bath' with a long vowel is correct in Bath but not in Seattle. 'Is it himself you're after speaking to?' may sound quaint in Brooklyn but could be everyday speech in Kerry. What looks from one viewpoint like poetry, in the sense of language intensely aware of itself, may be another person's ordinary speech. Language which is archaic often sounds poetic to us, but may well not have done so to its original users.

3.2 Estrangement

The Formalists, then, recognised that literariness, or what they called the poetic function, was not a thing in itself, eternally fixed and objectively isolable, but a relation between different kinds of discourse. The poetic is the function of a difference between kinds of language, not an immutable set of properties. It is a matter of self-referential signs; but what counts as this changes from place to place and time to time. Even so, it is not always clear with the Formalists what exactly is being estranged. Is it the word (or signifier) itself; the idea (or signified); or the object (or referent) to which the word refers? Do we come away from the poem with a refreshed sense of the phrase 'Golden Gate Bridge', or of the concept, or of the actual structure itself? The general idea, anyway, is clear: poetry is a kind of creative abnormality, an exhilarating illness of language – rather as, when we are actually ill and so cease to take our bodies for granted, we have an unwelcome opportunity to experience them afresh.

In arguing all this, the Formalists boldly offered what they saw as a universal theory of poetry; but it is a theory which clearly belongs to a certain kind of civilisation. Generally speaking, it stems from the kind of social order in which language has become excessively pragmatic and instrumental. Poetry is really a kind of spiritual therapy for those moderns whose words have withered, whose speech has become as bland and flavourless as their food, and whose experience has been drearily routinised. It is the poetics of a social order governed by utility – one in which everything appears to exist purely for the sake of something else, and in which our senses have grown calloused and anaesthetised. ('Anaesthetic', which means 'unfeeling', is the opposite of 'aesthetic', a word which originally refers not to art but to sensation and perception.) Formalism is the poetics of an alienated society – and its response to this condition, ironically, is to alienate the alienation. It estranges our automated language and experience so that we can begin to live and feel them anew. Two negatives make a positive.

It is worth noting, then, that Formalism, like so much of modernist theory, is a negative aesthetics – one that defines poetry not by any positive features it might exhibit, but by its difference or deviation from something else. The poetic is constituted by what it bounces off against, and so is dependent on the very alienated reality to which it is a response. It is not obvious what Virgil, Dante or Milton would have made of this account of what they were up to. It also implies, questionably, that creativity is nowhere to be found in everyday language and experience; it is, rather, the privileged preserve of whatever resists them. There is a smack of elitism about this doctrine, even though several of the Formalists were Bolshevik fellow travellers. This 'radical' scepticism of the common life has raised its head again in our own time, in the postmodern assumption that the creative is to be found only in margins and minorities, in the deviant and anti-consensual.

Formalist critics like Viktor Shklovsky, Boris Eichenbaum and Roman Jakobson argued that the function of estrangement was common to all literary devices. This is an astonishingly audacious claim. If it is true, then these theorists really have stumbled upon the literary equivalent of the philosopher's stone. They have achieved what no other literary critic in history has managed to do: namely, to show what rhyme and plot, repetition and dramatic irony, assonance, metaphor, narrative structure and so on all have in common. It is a marvellously imaginative notion, and the fact that it is not true should not be allowed to obscure its resourcefulness. Estrangement in Formalist hands becomes an admirably versatile notion. It succeeds in explain-

of 'beauty', as well as the *i* of 'terrible', is echoed in the vowel-sound of the word 'is'. Then, however, as though the line is in danger of becoming too tediously uniform, we have that intrusive 'born', with its insertion of a very different vowel-sound. Even so, the *r* of 'born' picks up on the *rr* of 'terrible', which binds the line more tightly together. (In Yeats's Hiberno-English idiom, the *r* sound would be accentuated more than it is in standard English.) One reason why the line works, then, is because phonically speaking it sets up a subtly modulated interplay of identity and difference. But it also pleases the ear rhythmically, consisting as it does of an iamb and two anapaests. (An iamb has one stressed and one unstressed syllable, while an anapaest consists of two unstressed syllables followed by one stressed one – *di-di-dum*.)[4] This is an interestingly complex, varied foot, neither too heavy nor too tripping; and having two of them side by side makes for a kind of balance and symmetry gratifying to the ear, as the line seems to pivot somewhere between the two.

In Lotman's view, a good literary work is one rich in information; and information is a matter of deviation. The more stable, predictable elements of a text, such as metre, belong to what one might call its dominant code. But because they are so regular, they tend also to be less perceptible. These are known to information theory as 'redundant' elements, which are necessary for conveying information but not in themselves informative. Think, for example, of the letters of the alphabet, which are meaningless in themselves but a necessary medium of meaning. The text is at its most informative when it deviates unpredictably from one of its codes, creating effects which stand out against this uniform background.

An example of this can be found in the first stanza of Robert Lowell's magnificent poem 'Mr. Edwards and the Spider':

> I saw the spiders marching through the air,
>   Swimming from tree to tree that mildewed day
>   In latter August when the hay
>   Came creaking to the barn. But where
>   The wind is westerly,
>   Where gnarled November makes the spiders fly
>   Into the apparitions of the sky,
>   They purpose nothing but their ease and die
>   Urgently beating east to sunrise and the sea . . .

---

[4] Though it should be said that this kind of thing is never an exact science. There are other ways of scanning the line.

We begin with two iambic pentameters, which sets up the expectation that this metrical form will continue; but lines 3 and 4 shift unpredictably into iambic tetrameters, lopping of a metrical foot, while line 5, an iambic trimeter, lops off yet another. Having shrunk around its waistline, so to speak, the stanza then begins to expand again into pentameters. The final line, however, is an alexandrine (six iambic feet), a traditional way of ending a stanza which provides yet another unforeseen twist to it.

Part of the surprise of the stanza is that its metre and rhyme are a good deal more formal than its language. The homely image of the hay creaking to the barn, where the imaginative masterstroke of 'creaking' redeems what might otherwise prove too banal a phrase, comes wrapped within a highly sophisticated manipulation of metre. What is creaking is presumably the wagon in which the hay is loaded; but since the poem does not actually say this, we are free to indulge the imaginative conceit that the hay itself is creaking. There is the sudden drama of an abrupt break in the line, followed by those two terse words 'But where', and then the hurried step across to the next line to sustain the sense, a line which turns out to be arrestingly short ('The wind is westerly'). It is as though form suddenly thrusts itself upon us, as we are made aware of the poet's need to conform his otherwise unostentatious language to the stringent requirements of rhyme and metre. 'Mildewed' day, a phrase in which the *d* in 'mildewed' discreetly echoes the *d* of 'day', is a particularly deft touch.

Dropping a metrical foot or two, as Lowell does in the verse, is what Lotman would describe as a 'minus device', meaning that our expectations are disrupted by something which we expect to appear but doesn't. So unpredictability can include the absence of an element as well as its presence. A rather more dramatic disruption of expectations occurs in the following limerick – one, appropriately enough, whose theme is poetic metre:

> There was a young poet of Japan
> Whose verses never would scan;
> When they asked him why, he said 'It's 'cos I
> Just can't help getting as many words into the last line as I possibly possibly can.'

Information, then, springs from deviation, and deviation requires the regularity of a code. The poetic for Lotman just is this alternation between the random and the regular carried to a point of well-nigh bottomless complexity. Indeed, in his view poetry is the most complex form of discourse imaginable. The puzzle would seem to be that a poem is the most 'semantically saturated' form of writing we have, yielding more information in a condensed space than any other kind of text; but that this in normal circumstances would run the risk of an informational overload. For information theory, too great an increase in information means a decrease in communication, as there is too much material for us to digest. Poetry, however, appears at once semantically saturated (crammed with meaning) and entirely communicable. Yet it is very low on 'redundancy', since it is the kind of text in which every element counts. How can this be so?

The answer lies in what Lotman has argued already about a poem's unique mode of organisation. A poetic text is rich in information because each of its elements, as we have seen, is located at the intersection of several overlaid systems. Each unit, if you like, is a kind of switching mechanism between a host of systems and sub-systems. It participates in several different systems simultaneously; and this is greatly complicated by the fact that every feature of a poem also leads a double life as both 'paradigmatic' and 'syntagmatic'. (The former term refers to the total pattern of the text, grasped as a spatial whole, while the latter refers to the relations set up 'laterally', as the poem moves forward line by line through time.) Each of these systems represents a norm from which the others diverge. Each system 'defamiliarises' the others, breaking up their regularity and throwing them into more vivid relief. Just as one system threatens to become too routinised and monotonous, another cuts across it to disrupt it into newly palpable presence.

It is as though a poem is a constant invasion of system by system, in which one system momentarily provides the norm and another the transgression, in a constantly shifting pattern. It involves a continual generating and violating of norms or expectations. Each system contains its own internal tensions, parallelisms, oppositions and so on, and each is constantly at work modifying the others. If, say, two words are associated by their sound, or by their place in the metrical scheme, this will also tend to yoke their meanings together; but it may also highlight their differences of meaning, so that the poem's semantic system disrupts its metrical or phonic ones. In doing so, it produces an increase in information. Since any two words in the text may be allied on some basis or another, these possibilities are effectively endless. How, we might then ask, does a poet accomplish all this without the aid of a computer? The answer is that he relies on his ear, rather as a tennis player relies not on aerodynamics but on her reflexes.

So a poem is an unfathomably complex interplay of systems. Because this interplay can never be predicted, it is rich in information; but because we are speaking of *systems* here, we are also speaking of regularity, and thus of communicability. It is the overlaying and interacting of systems which produce both information and communication. What deviates from one system is another system; and this both produces information and preserves communication. In Lotman's eyes, it also provides a basis for evaluation. Good poems are those rich in information. Whereas Keats claimed that truth was beauty, Lotman maintains that information is.

Attending to the systemic nature of poems should not blind us to the fact that they are also examples of play. This is another way in which they stand askew to a civilisation obsessed by business. Simply by existing, poetry fulfils a utopian function, testifying to a form of life which would be less in thrall to labour, coercion and obligation. Poets, like infants, relish sounds for their own sake. Poetry is a superior form of babbling. The most lofty exercises of the imagination, as we have seen, border on the most regressive of fantasies. A poem is a piece of semiotic sport, in which the signifier has been momentarily released from its grim communicative labours and can disport itself disgracefully. Freed from a loveless marriage to a single meaning, it can play the field, wax promiscuous, gambol outrageously with similar unattached signifiers. If the guardians of conventional morality knew what scandalous stuff they were inscribing on their tombstones, they would cease to do so immediately.

Play is the opposite of instrumental activity, even though it performs a vital role in our development. One problem with that development, according to the psychoanalytical theories of Jacques Lacan, is that the small infant can never really distinguish what is being done to it for instrumental or utilitarian reasons from what is not. Being fed, washed and kept warm by its carers is in fact an act of love on their part; but for Lacan this expression of love is experienced by the infant as troublingly ambiguous, since it can never appear purely as itself.[5] Instead, it must inevitably be obscured by the functional form it takes. What the infant demands is to be recognised in its own right; but it can never be entirely sure how to recognise such recognition. In Lacanian theory, it is in this gap between the demand for unconditional recognition and the satisfaction of pragmatic need that desire, or the unconscious, first germinates. To play with infants, however, is to do nothing other than to recognise them for what they are, with no ulterior goal in mind. It is in play that we come into our own as human subjects. And poetry is among other things a memory-trace of this primordial sense of being accepted for what we are.

[5] For an account of Lacan's thought, see Terry Eagleton, *Literary Theory: An Introduction* (Oxford, 1983), Ch. 5.

3.4   The Incarnational Fallacy

Lotman emphasises that each system in a poem is semi-autonomous of the others; and this is a point which many critics have damagingly overlooked. Instead, they have sought for a theory of the work which sees each of its aspects as harmoniously integrated with the rest. Prominent in this kind of approach has been what we might call the 'incarnational fallacy'. On this view, form and content in poetry are entirely at one because the poem's language somehow 'incarnates' its meaning. Whereas everyday language simply points to things, poetic language actually embodies them. There is a theology lurking behind this poetics: just as the Word of God is the Father made flesh, so a poem does not simply talk about things, but in some mysterious way 'becomes' them. This sacramental view of signs is to be found, among many other places, in T. S. Eliot's *Four Quartets*, though it crops up there in bleakly negative guise: poetry, with its intolerable wrestle with words and meanings, can never attain the fullness of presence of the Incarnation. Words can never attain the status of the Word. Language can intimate truth by drawing attention to its own limits, and thus to what transcends them; or it can yield a negative insight into truth by cancelling itself out; but in a fallen world it cannot capture it in the flesh. It is a quintessentially modernist motif.

A rather eccentric example of the incarnational fallacy can be found in F. R. Leavis's comments on the phrase 'moss'd cottage trees' in Keats's ode 'To Autumn':

> The action of the packed consonants in 'moss'd cottage trees' is plain enough: there stand the trees, gnarled and sturdy in trunk and bough, their leafy entanglements thickly loaded. It is not fanciful, I think, to find that (the sense being what it is) the pronouncing of 'cottage-trees' suggests, too, the crisp bite and the flow of juice as the teeth close in the ripe apple.[6]

If this is not fanciful, it is hard to know what is. It is 'plain' to Leavis that we can see the gnarled, sturdy trees with their thickly loaded leafy entanglements, though the poem says nothing of this. This is rather like claiming that it is plain that Hamlet has freckles and a broken nose.

For Leavis, genuine poetic language is as packed and ripe as an apple, and reading becomes rather like chewing. Words are at their most authentic when

---

[6]   F. R. Leavis, *The Common Pursuit* (Harmondsworth, 1962), p. 16.

they are plumped with the ripe physicality of things. Pressed to an extreme, this means that the truest poet would be a greengrocer. In seeking to do homage to words, revering them as densely physical objects in their own right, the incarnational fallacy only succeeds in abolishing them. For words which 'become' what they signify cease to be words at all. At their most material, they disappear into the objects they are supposed to denote. For all its celebration of the muscularity of language, the incarnational fallacy reflects a covert distrust of it. Only when words cease to be themselves and merge into their referents can they be truly expressive. Leavis believes that English speech is naturally incarnational, whereas ill-starred foreigners like the French have to make do with an inferior kind of language altogether, one which palely reflects things rather than concretely enacts them. This linguistic Little Englandism is one of the more absurd aspects of an astonishingly courageous and pioneering critic.

Seamus Heaney's 'Digging' may illustrate the point:

> . . . The coarse boot nestled on the lug, the shaft
> Against the inside knee was levered firmly,
> He rooted out tall tops, buried the bright edge deep
> To scatter new potatoes that we picked
> Loving their cool hardness in our hands . . .
>
> The cold smell of potato mould, the squelch and slap
> Of soggy peat, the curt cuts of an edge
> Through living roots awaken in my head . . .

This intensely physical language seems the outward expression of the poem's subject matter, as form and content appear to melt into one another. The 'curt cuts' of the spade are also the curt cuts of a language which admits only two trisyllabic words, and one of these is the lowly, palpable 'potato'. Otherwise we get a chain of elemental, bluntly expressive monosyllables: 'coarse', 'lug', 'shaft', 'mould', 'squelch', 'slap', 'curt', most of them redolent of earth, mud and moisture. So the language seems to incarnate what it speaks of. Like the digger himself, it appears to be rammed right up against the coarse grains and textures of the world, rather than floating loftily above them. It is as though the words absorb into their own bodies the bitter soil and mould of which they speak, to the point where it is hard to slide even the thickness of a hair between signifier, signified and referent.

Compare these lines, then, with the first verse of Rupert Brooke's famously patriotic 'The Soldier':

If I should die, think only this of me:
  That there's some corner of a foreign field
That is for ever England. There shall be
  In that rich earth a richer dust concealed;
A dust whom England bore, shaped, made aware,
  Gave, once, her flowers to love, her ways to roam,
A body of England's, breathing English air,
  Washed by the rivers, blest by suns of home.

This, too, is about the earth, but it scarcely smacks of it. On the contrary, its fervent, edifying tone tends to obscure just how abstract and non-particularised a poem it is – as in that very notional 'her flowers to love, her ways to roam', which could have come straight from a greetings card in a way that Heaney's 'squelch and slap of soggy peat' could not. 'Earth' and 'dust' for Brooke have a purely symbolic value, which is by no means a defect in itself. Poems can be symbolically generalised, indifferent to the density of actual things, without losing anything of their persuasive force. But if dust is what we are made of, then dying can be made to sound like merging effortlessly back into our native element, and so can have the sting and messiness taken out of it. It is an understandable fantasy to indulge in for a soldier in the First World War.

Yet the difference between the two kinds of language is fundamentally a *trompe l'oeil* or illusion. It is not that Heaney's language is actually closer to reality, while the more refined diction of the Brooke poem stands further off from it. Language and reality are not two objects like bookends, with variable distances between them. The language of 'Digging' is just as conceptual as the idealising phraseology of 'The Soldier'. This is because all language is conceptual, and making it seem otherwise is just a kind of poetic sleight of hand. It may feel as though the words of the Heaney poem somehow embody the very stuff they speak of, but what looks incarnational is really associational. We associate one kind of materiality – the blunt, unmelodious, coarse-grained sounds of 'lug', 'shaft', 'squelch' and so on – with another kind of materiality: the soil, spade, mud and vegetation which constitute the poem's subject matter. But the former kind of physicality does not 'embody' the latter. The two kinds of materiality are of quite different orders. One is a matter of the way certain words feel in our mouth, while the other is a question of natural processes. (It is not fanciful, perhaps, to suggest that the two converge in our unconscious memory in the form of one of our very earliest experiences: the gratifying taste of milk in our mouths.) The language moves at one level, and the subject matter at another; but we are persuaded to see them as stitched together as closely as a jacket and its lining.

Words like 'silk', 'softness' and 'murmur' are not usually regarded as 'earthy' because they slide easily from our mouths, requiring a minimum of labour. It is words we chew, bite on or spit out which we associate with the material world, since both demand a certain amount of labour. Words which are mouth-filling or recalcitrant tend to evoke material substances, since these substances, too, resist us in their heft and density. But a lot of these associations are purely fanciful. You may imagine that the word 'dank' has a dankish feel to it, but if this is to do with the vowel sound, why is 'prank' not similarly evocative? The word 'slimy' may sound slimy, but this is only because it means slimy.

We have come to forge magical associations between words and things, seeing them as necessarily bound up with one another. This, to adopt an image from the philosopher Ludwig Wittgenstein, is rather like marvelling at the way a word on a page seems to fit the space provided for it so exactly. We come to transfer some of the qualities of an object to the word that stands for it. It is what the critic Paul de Man called the 'phenomenalisation of language', an operation he associated with the wiles of ideology.[7] But we have only to look at languages other than English to puncture this delusion. 'Cow' may sound a blunt, inelegant sort of word, rather like the animal itself; but do we feel the same about *vache*? And how do the French feel about the matter?

There are two words in the Heaney poem which really do embody what they refer to, and those are 'squelch' and 'slap'. This is because both of them are onomatopoeic. They sound like what they signify. This, however, is about the only way that poems actually do 'incarnate' their meanings. And it is a very minor part of poetic business. We have seen already that poetry involves at least two things: a certain memorable or inventive use of language, and a moral insight into human existence. But most theories of poetry have come to grief on the question of how these are interrelated. The Formalists could reconcile them after a fashion, since renewing our language also meant refreshing our experience, and this, broadly speaking, is a moral process. But making the world more 'perceptible', more palpable to our senses, is moral only in a rather fuzzy sense of the word. It is not a matter of investigating human values and activities in depth, in the manner of Homer's *Iliad* or Arthur Hugh Clough's *Amours de Voyage*.

---

[7] See Paul de Man, *The Rhetoric of Romanticism* (New York, 1984).

The truth is that these two different dimensions of a poem – its language and its moral exploration – need not be internally related at all. (I mean by 'internal' a kind of logical or necessary relationship, such that the one entails the other.) What we might call the paradigmatic case of poetry is when they do indeed come together – when the pleasing, inventive, unusual or arresting use of words suddenly yields us a fresh insight into some experience or situation. Take these well-known lines by A. E. Housman from his volume *A Shropshire Lad*:

> Into my heart an air that kills
> From yon far country blows:
> What are those blue remembered hills,
> What spires, what farms are those?

The juxtaposition of 'blue' and 'remembered' is notable because the two adjectives seem so different – the first describing a material quality, the second concerning an act of consciousness. The physical and psychological are coupled casually together, as though they were the same sort of thing. Not putting a comma between them, as one might conventionally expect, enhances this effect. There is no practical association between the two terms, since it is not as though the poet is remembering that the hills are blue. The juxtaposition suggests rather that they are remembered in the same sense that they are blue. It evokes an equivalence between the two adjectives. Squeezed up against 'blue', 'remembered' comes to sound like a quality of the hills themselves, rather than a function of the poet's mind. The hills are 'remembered' rather as they are grassy or craggy. Because the line (an iambic tetrameter) is so short, it can accommodate only about half a dozen words; so the choice of 'blue' and 'remembered', out of all the fancier epithets Housman could have opted for, stands out fairly starkly. What is important about these hills is that they are remembered, as permanently and intensely as they are blue. They are remembered all over the place, just as they are blue from one end to another.

The line estranges the words 'blue' and 'remembered' both by choosing them when we feel it could have selected so many alternatives, and by letting each word rub the other into a new kind of palpability. 'Remembered' is an ordinary sort of term; but 'remember' is more often encountered in its verbal than adjectival form, so that its impact here is more forceful and jolting than we might otherwise expect. 'Well remembered' or 'lovingly remembered' would be predictable, but 'remembered' by itself is not. And 'blue' is striking in its monosyllabic simplicity. It is almost as though the poem is daring us to complain that it is too commonplace, a waste of an opportunity for some finer epithet. But it is the blueness of the hills which is precious.

So this would be an instance of the paradigmatically poetic: of an arresting piece of language which is at the same time a fresh kind of moral insight. Not all poetry, however, works like this all of the time. If a piece of writing had no striking verbal effects at all, and no moral insights, then it is doubtful we would call it a poem. But what if it *only* had striking verbal effects, like 'Jeepers, Creepers, where d'ya get those peepers?', or 'Di-dee-diddly-doo-de-dum-dee-dah'? ('Striking', as the reader may have gathered, does not necessarily mean 'deeply impressive'.) We might call this wordplay rather than poetry proper, rather as Freud distinguishes between jokes, which have a content, and jests, which are more concerned with the play of the signifier. Or what if the work displayed some powerful moral insights but verbally speaking was as dull as an income-tax return?

The truth, surely, is that we look to poetry both for a bravura of the signifier and a depth and subtlety of the signified. But it is asking too much to expect these things always to happen precisely in terms of each other, and theories of poetry which stake themselves on such notions of unity bite off more than they can chew. Faced with Robert Frost's 'My little horse must think it queer / To stop without a farmhouse near', we reap a modest pleasure from the tripping of the metre and the rhyming of 'queer' and 'near', as we do from the idea which the lines proffer to us. It is amusing and mildly illuminating to think of a horse behaving like a taxi-driver and wondering whether his stopping is scheduled or random. But there is no sense in which the two effects, one of form and one of content, are inseparable. Frost could presumably have formulated the same idea with another rhyme. Poetic language, after all, is not as inevitable and unalterable as some commentators imagine. Nor are the kinds of satisfaction we glean from these two dimensions of the poem at all similar. There is a pleasure of the signifier and a pleasure of moral cognition, but it is excessively 'organicist' to imagine that the one always operates in terms of the other. If this is what Keats meant by claiming that beauty was truth and truth beauty, then he was, dare one suggest, mistaken.

In the last two chapters we have examined some theoretical questions about the nature of poetry. It is now time to put these to the test by looking at poetic form in action.

Chapter 4

In Pursuit of Form

4.1 The Meaning of Form

Roughly speaking, what we call content refers to what a poem says, while form refers to how it says it. Most critics would want to insist that these two aspects of the work are inseparable. In fact, this doctrine is as well-entrenched with literary critics as a belief in witches was with the Inquisition. Pushed to an extreme, it becomes mildly ridiculous, as when critics claim to hear the rustling of the silk in the hissing of the *s* sounds. This is known as the mimetic theory of form, for which the form somehow imitates the content it expresses. Alexander Pope admonishes us in his poem *An Essay on Criticism* that in poetry 'the sound must seem an echo to the sense', though some examples of this he finds rather silly. The alexandrine, for instance, 'That, like a wounded snake, drags its slow length along'.

If it is true in one sense that form and content are inseparable, it is false in another. It is true, as they say, 'existentially' – true as far as our actual experience of the poem goes. When we read John Milton's words 'Eyeless in Gaza at the mill with slaves', we do not hear or see a distinction between form and content. But we recognise a conceptual distinction between them even so, just as we recognise a conceptual distinction between the evening star and the morning star, even though they are existentially speaking one and the same (the planet Venus). This is what philosophers refer to as an analytical rather than a real distinction. Form and content may be inseparable in experience; but the very fact that we use two different terms here suggests that they are not identical. Literary forms have a history of their own; they are not just the obedient expression of content.

W. B. Yeats, with this dichotomy, among others, in mind, asked in a poem how we could tell the dancer from the dance; and it is true that this is hard to do while the dance is actually in progress. A dancer just is someone who dances, and a dance is just the way a dancer moves. Even so, Yeats's claim is truer of modern-day dancing than it is of the old-fashioned ball-room variety. It is truer of the kind of dance which you improvise on the spot than of waltzes and foxtrots, which clearly have some notional existence distinguishable from dancers themselves. If they didn't, nobody could ever learn them.

Form concerns such aspects of the poem as tone, pitch, rhythm, diction, volume, metre, pace, mood, voice, address, texture, structure, quality, syntax, register, point of view, punctuation and the like, whereas content is a matter of meaning, action, character, idea, storyline, moral vision, argument and so on. ('Form' is sometimes used in a narrow sense as synonymous with 'struc-ture' or 'design', meaning the way the various elements of a literary work relate to one other; but there is no reason to restrict the term to this.) In one sense, these two dimensions of form and content are obviously distinct. We can speak, for example, of two poems sharing the same metre or even much the same mood. Or we can speak of them as using the same devices of assonance or alliteration, without implying that the poems in question are one and the same. What the two poems 'say' with the aid of these strategies is clearly different. We can also, for example, distinguish in fiction between narrative and narration – the former referring to the storyline, the latter meaning the way the story gets told. The same narrative can be narrated in different ways.

The distinction between form and content is notoriously leaky. Mood and tone, for example, are aspects of what we might call semantic content – of a specific pattern of meaning – from which they cannot really be dissociated. Even so, the distinction can be a useful one. You can write a history of lit-erary forms – of types of allegory, for example, or the use of the Chorus in drama, or first-person narration – which doesn't attend in exhaustive detail to the content of particular works; or you can produce a history of the bicycle in literature which cuts across works which have very different formal properties. You can discuss a piece of poetry in terms of form – say, how it handles irony or metaphor or ambiguity; or you may be more interested in the actual meanings at stake in the irony, metaphor or ambiguity, in which case you are looking at content. Discussing the character of Elizabeth Bennet in *Pride and Prejudice* is a matter of content (of 'what?'), whereas examining Jane Austen's techniques of characterisation is a question of form (or 'how?'). Some may find these fine distinctions scholastic, but then some find any fine distinctions scholastic.

Yet form and content are inseparable in this sense – that literary criticism typically involves grasping *what* is said in terms of *how* it is said. Or, to put it slightly more technically, grasping the semantic (meaning) in terms of the non-semantic (sound, rhythm, structure, typography and so on). Of course readers will sometimes want to attend more to the one, and sometimes more to the other. You may be more concerned for the moment with examining sexual passion in *Wuthering Heights*, which roughly speaking is a matter of content, than with the novel's use of so-called unreliable narrators like Lockwood and Nelly Dean, which is largely a question of form. Not every critical statement has to be a what-in-terms-of-how one. It can be claimed, however, that the *prototypical* act of criticism is just this. And this seems to be true above all of poetry – a literary genre which could almost be defined as one in which form and content are intimately interwoven. It is as though poetry above all discloses the secret truth of all literary writing: that form is *constitutive* of content and not just a reflection of it. Tone, rhythm, rhyme, syntax, assonance, grammar, punctuation and so on are actually generators of meaning, not just containers of it. To modify any of them is to modify meaning itself.

But isn't this equally true of everyday language? What's so special about literature here? The tone in which I address my 'Good morning' to you, whether frosty or fawning, can make a dramatic difference to its meaning. Whole dialogues have been composed by taking a single obscenity and repeating it a number of times, each time inflecting it in a different tone. This kind of thing may not have the grandeur of *War and Peace*, but it makes a point even so. Tone, pace, pitch and the like may help to constitute the sense of what I say in ordinary life as well as in poetry. I am telling you that it is three minutes past six in this orotund, absurdly emphatic way in order to convey the fact that I regard you as a pest who ought to have the decency to buy your own watch. An ironic or sarcastic tone can actually reverse the meaning of what I say. Making sense in everyday life is a matter of the way we use signs which are meaningless in themselves according to certain agreed conventions; and this is another way of saying that the content of our speech is determined by its form. Individual words have a purely formal existence, as is clear from the fact that 'pig' and *cochon* have the same meaning.

So there is no clean break here between literature and life. It is true that a great deal of poetry exploits the resources of language more intensively than most of our everyday speech, unless one happens to be Oscar Wilde.

(Even here, however, we should be on our guard: some poems are plain and austere, while some everyday utterances can be florid and profuse.) But poetry also puts on show what is true about our language anyway, but which goes generally unnoticed. In everyday language, too, 'content' is the product of 'form'. Or, to put it more technically, signifieds (meanings) are a product of signifiers (words). Meanings are a matter of how we use words, rather than words being a matter of conveying meanings which are formed independently of them. I could not have the idea 'Tigers should be frolicked with wherever possible' unless I had words or signs to have it in. In daily life, however, we are mostly content analysts, reading for meaning rather than form. We stare right through the signifier to what it signifies. We do not generally point out to the butcher with a cry of triumph that he has just come up with two alliterations and an anapaest.

So it is as though poetry grants us the actual experience of seeing meaning take shape as a practice, rather than handling it simply as a finished object. Or, if you like, seeing form take shape as content, a process which for most of time we mercifully don't notice. 'Mercifully', because this insensitivity to the texture and rhythm of our speech is essential to our practical lives. There is no point in shouting 'Fire!' in a cinema if the audience are simply going to linger over the delectable contrast between the violently stabbing *F* and the swooning, long-drawn-out vowel. (Those among the audience disadvantaged by an old-style literary education might even detect in this verbal performance a mimetic image of the fire itself: the *F* representing its abrupt beginnings, and the swooning vowel the rush and roll of its inexorable spreading. . . .)

Just as it looks as though the sun moves round the earth, so ordinary language seems to invert the relations between signifiers and signifieds, or words and their meanings. In everyday speech, it seems as though the word is simply the obedient transmitter of the meaning. It is as though it evaporates into it. If language did not conceal its operations in this way, we might be so enraptured by its music that, like the Lotus Eaters, we would never get anything done – rather as for Nietzsche, if we were mindful of the appalling butchery which produced civilised humanity, we would never get out of bed. Ordinary language, like history for Nietzsche or the ego for Freud, operates by a kind of salutary amnesia or repression. Poetry is the kind of writing which stands this inversion of form and content, or signifier and signified, on its feet again. It makes it hard for us to brush aside the words to get at the meanings. It makes it clear that the signified is the result of a complex play of signifiers. And in doing so, it allows us to experience the very medium of our experience.

form leads us to expect simplicity, but which in fact conceals a complex content. Take, for example, that desperately enigmatic narrative, 'Three Blind Mice':

> Three blind mice, three blind mice,
> See how they run, see how they run.
> They all ran after the farmer's wife,
> She cut off their tails with a carving knife,
> Did you ever see such a thing in your life
> As three blind mice?

It is hard to unravel exactly what is going on here. Are the mice of the first two lines running *away* from the farmer's wife because she has cut off their tails, or are they running *after* her? Does the verse describe two actions or one? One possible chronology of events is that the farmer's wife cut off the tails of three mice who were running after her, an act which somehow blinded them (the connection here is admittedly obscure, but there are undertones of castration), thus causing them to take fright and run away from her. This would account for the shift of tense from present to past: the narrative opens with an event in the present, then backtracks to highlight its past cause.

But one could also read the verse as a single action in the present: three mice, already blind, are running after the farmer's wife, who cuts off their tails. This, admittedly, fails to account for the change of tense, and it is hard to see how the mice could run after the farmer's wife if they were blind; but otherwise it is a reasonably plausible reading. If one opts for the first interpretation, a certain ironic reversal is detectable, of which the nub is the shift from line 2 to line 3: the mice who previously scampered so gleefully in pursuit of the farmer's wife are now fleeing, panic-stricken, away from her. Nobody comes out of the piece particularly well, not least the sadistic speaker.

Some poems mean one thing by what they say, and another, perhaps contradictory thing by the way they say it. William Empson, for example, brilliantly demonstrates in his study *Some Versions of Pastoral* how a verse in Thomas Gray's 'Elegy in a Country Churchyard' involves just this sort of ambiguity:

> Full many a gem of purest ray serene
> The dark, unfathomed caves of ocean bear;
> Full many a flower is born to blush unseen
> And waste its sweetness on the desert air.

The lines are meant to illustrate the pathos of the fact that some bright people are held back by their obscure origins from attaining worldly fame. But as

Empson points out, the elegance of the verse dignifies this dire situation in a way which makes us feel reluctant to see it altered. By comparing it to a natural condition, it also makes it seem as though it could not in fact be altered. Intellectually ambitious farm labourers presumably object to the poverty which holds them back; but as Empson points out, gems do not mind being in caves, and flowers prefer not to be plucked. The imagery is askew to the argument it is meant to underpin. 'Blush', Empson speculates, carries a resonance of virginity, and so a suggestion that renunciation is desirable, including perhaps the kind of sacrifice forced upon talented people from modest social backgrounds.

There are also poems, however, in which an elaborateness of form conceals a paucity of content. Dylan Thomas's 'A Refusal to Mourn the Death, by Fire, of a Child in London' is a case in point:

> Never until the mankind making
> Bird beast and flower
> Fathering and all humbling darkness
> Tells with silence the last light breaking
> And the still hour
> Is come of the sea tumbling in harness
>
> And I must enter again the round
> Zion of the water bead
> And the synagogue of the ear of corn
> Shall I let pray the shadow of a sound
> Or sow my salt seed
> In the least valley of sackcloth to mourn
>
> The majesty and burning of the child's death.
> I shall not murder
> The mankind of her going with a grave truth
> Nor blaspheme down the stations of the breath
> With any further
> Elegy of innocence and youth.
>
> Deep with the first dead lies London's daughter,
> Robed in the long friends,
> The grains beyond age, the dark veins of her mother,
> Secret by the unmourning water
> Of the riding Thames.
> After the first death, there is no other.

This goes to extraordinary lengths to say astonishingly little. Thomas's rhetoric is impressive in its excessively high-pitched way, but if you strip away the sonorously ceremonial language, the poem falls to pieces. The pseudo-scriptural imagery, some of which is tellingly original and inventive, is really there to pad out a central emptiness, diverting attention from the fact that the poem has little to say about the burnt child, and even less sympathy for her. Its language moves at one level and its subject matter at another. The whole first half of the piece is a kind of extended metaphorical riff on the word 'Never', the imagery of which is largely at a tangent to the poem's official subject, and the whole of which concerns the poet himself (and his artistic virtuosity) rather than the dead victim.

The reader has to wait ten lines, until the arrival of the main verb 'Shall I let pray', to see what this 'Never' clause is modifying, as though the poet is so absorbed in his own metaphorical pyrotechnics that he comes near to losing track of what he was about to say. This, we shall soon learn, is because he has embarrassingly little to say in the first place. The child is a mere occasion for baroque image-spinning. It is as though the fact that she is a corpse, rather than a living individual, can be used to rationalise her purely notional status in these verses. To treat her as an impersonal symbol or mythological archetype, the poem seems to insinuate, is somehow a deeper insight than to see her as an actual person. The whole piece is flagrantly opportunistic. It is the orotund rhetoric of the clause beginning with 'Never', with all its freewheeling metaphorical fertility, which the poet invests in most deeply, not the substantive statement which it is supposed to be modifying. The poem is actually built out of this imbalance of form and content, one which it seems brazenly to flaunt.

When the piece finally gets round to the girl, which isn't until the last stanza, it manages to make indifference sound like wisdom. 'The majesty and burning of the child's death', a line meant to dignify its subject, simply succeeds in making being burnt to death sound noble. 'I shall not murder / The mankind of her going with a grave truth' sounds impressively candid and tough-minded: other may perfume this death with their moral platitudes, but Thomas himself, who is laying pontifical claim to the high moral ground here, defiantly refuses to play along with this hypocritical bombast. The only problem is that the very language in which he rejects this posturing is itself rhetorical posturing. 'Grave truth' is a cheap pun.

The 'mankind' of the child's death presumably means that death is natural to humanity, and so not an occasion for mourning (though Thomas maintains just the opposite in a poem about the death of his father). But 'mankind' is too close to 'humaneness' for comfort, and one suspects in any case that it is there largely to alliterate with the typically hyperbolic flourish of 'murder'. The last thing Thomas's language is is candid. Its *gravitas* and ornate solemnity make his refusal to mourn seem somehow profound, as though he has divined a truth beyond the shallow perceptions of others. The last stanza finally discloses that truth, which turns out to be a piece of reach-me-down Nature mysticism. Mother Earth has taken her daughter back to her bosom, and since the Thames isn't mourning, why should we? 'After the first death, there is no other', for all its grave air of prophetic insight, is uncomfortably close to 'Once you've seen one, you've seen the lot.'

There is also a use of poetic form which seems to detach it from the content in order to make an implicit comment on it. The famous seduction-of-the-typist scene in T. S. Eliot's *The Waste Land* might serve as an illustration:

> He, the young man carbuncular, arrives,
> A small house agent's clerk, with one bold stare,
> One of the low on whom assurance sits
> As a silk hat on a Bradford millionaire.
> The time is now propitious, as he guesses,
> The meal is ended, she is bored and tired,
> Endeavours to engage her in caresses
> Which still are unreproved, if undesired.
> Flushed and decided, he assaults at once;
> Exploring hands encounter no defence;
> His vanity requires no response,
> And makes a welcome of indifference . . .

The iambic pentameters fall with a kind of jaded, you-know-the-sort-of-thing sophistication, as the sordid scene unfurls itself with a kind of weary fatalism. (The famous opening line of the poem, incidentally – 'April is the cruellest month, breeding . . .' – is a kind of broken-backed pentameter, a frail ghost of what was once a robust literary form). The loveless, mechanical sex is reflected in the pat, automated stresses of the lines. The ritualised beat of the rhymes and rhythms seems to point up the squalid predictability of the whole affair. The poetry seems bored by what it is narrating, superciliously holding its nose and trying to put as much distance between itself and its own subject matter as it can. 'One of the low', 'propitious', 'As a silk hat on a Bradford millionaire': these are all phrases which rise distastefully above the scene, disdaining it in the act of observing it.

The language of the piece is nothing like the kind of idiom which the typist and the clerk would use themselves, though it has been suggested

faintly rebarbative, in order to throw a final flattering light on the sensuality being left behind. There is also, perhaps, a slightly schoolmasterish feel to the admonition 'all neglect', as though a spot of finger-wagging is going on here. But the poem gets away with it.

Yeats is not the kind of writer who explores nature in Keatsian or Hopkinsian detail. There is nothing lavish, profuse or sensuously detailed about the birds in the trees, the salmon-falls and the mackerel-crowded seas. 'Fish, flesh, or fowl' sounds more like a grocer's terminology than a poet's. 'Mackerel-crowded' is a fine stroke, and 'mackerel' (if the pun may be forgiven) a splendidly mouth-filling word; but 'the young in one another's arms' and 'birds in the trees' are deliberately bare and notational. It is as though Yeats is just touching them in on his poetic canvas, without the least intent to lend them complex, convincing life. They are little more than emblems, like (for the most part) the swan in 'Coole Park and Ballylee'.

Yet the poem's achievement is to create the *effect* of lavishness and profuseness from these few meagre, economical items, an effect which would have taken Gerard Manley Hopkins at least another dozen lines. The stanza generates a cornucopian sense of abundance out of the sparsest of materials. And whereas one feels that Hopkins might have been carried away by this potentially inexhaustible fertility, Yeats remains rigorously in control, as the orderly syntax suggests. By about line 4, we are growing a little anxious: what are all these bits and pieces adding up to? Then, suddenly, a main verb ('commend') locks authoritatively into place in the next line, to bind these various elements together and lend them some overall thrust and coherence.

It is as though the chain of brief phrases, with its rapid, cumulative build-up, generates a sense of mounting excitement, one those young lovers might find familiar. Its grammatical open-endedness suggests that this copious piling of life-form upon life-form could in principle go on forever, creating just the sense of exuberance and prodigality that the verse is after. But that clinching main verb, not to speak of the beautifully intricate rhyme scheme, is on hand to assure us that everything is under control. It is as though Yeats's breathing-in, in preparation for the delayed arrival of the main verb, has been deep enough to allow him to voice one brief phrase after another ('the salmon-falls, the mackerel-crowded seas . . .') without things getting out of hand. So the intellect is not just in Byzantium, to be encountered on disembarking, but is already unobtrusively at work in the present. The exclamatory excitement of the lines, with their staccato rhythms, hint at the possibility of an ecstatic loss of control in the face of these fleshly delights, without ever coming remotely close to it.

In 'A Disused Shed in Co. Wexford', a later Irish poet, Derek Mahon, demonstrates a masterly dominance of form over content. Here is the final stanza or so of the poem, which daringly compares a crowd of fetid mushrooms trapped in the darkness of a shed to concentration-camp victims. The metaphor is breathtakingly bold, not least because it courts the danger of dignifying the mushrooms only at the cost of devaluing the victims:

> . . . Grown beyond nature now, soft food for worms,
> They lift frail heads in gravity and good faith.
> They are begging us, you see, in their wordless way,
> To do something, to speak on their behalf
> Or at least not to close the door again.
> Lost people of Treblinka and Pompeii!
> 'Save us, save us', they seem to say,
> 'Let the god not abandon us
> Who have come so far in darkness and in pain.
> We too had our lives to live.
> You with your light meter and relaxed itinerary,
> Let not our naïve labours have been in vain!'

The build-up to this last stanza is full of grotesque, nightmarish imagery, as the 'web-throated' mushrooms, racked by draught, groan piteously for their deliverance. Yet just as the agony grows well-nigh intolerable, that formal, scrupulously well-turned line 'They lift frail heads in gravity and good faith' intervenes with its double alliteration, so that what follows is not a panic-stricken scramble of rotting mushrooms but a dignified, sombrely eloquent appeal. The poem, too, asserts its control, calmly refusing to lose its head. As the door swings open to reveal this almost unbearable pathos, the speaker needs to retain his poise because this is now the moment when he must speak out on behalf of these wordless creatures, ventriloquising their agony through his own verse. He is not shocked spectator but interpreter, rather like the interpreters whom those who liberated the Nazi death camps would no doubt have had in tow. It devolves on the poet to explain to those too traumatised or distraught to grasp this horror precisely what is going on, inserting an almost pedantic 'you see' into his commentary like a conscientious guide.

In the teeth of this appalling spectacle, the poem continues in its unruffled way to analyse and qualify: note that 'Or *at least* not to close the door again', and the complex verb of the final line. This is not the kind of thing that the mushrooms themselves could say, but there is a kind of courteous pretence that they could ('they *seem* to say'), one which restores to them some of their lost dignity. 'Who have come so far in darkness and in pain' is not only an iambic pentameter but is meant to be perceptible to us as such. Even in this state of extremity, language continues to rebuff silence, to the point where the verse can venture what could almost be a piece of elegant, Audenesque wit or irony: 'You with your light meter and relaxed itinerary'. The studied, self-conscious artifice of this line is far beyond the capability of the tormented mushrooms themselves; but once more the poem hands it to them, so to speak, as a kind of gift, lending them something its own poise and eloquence.

Note, finally, that line 'Lost people of Treblinka and Pompeii!', which seems to hang by itself in the stanza. It has no grammatical link to anything around it, occurring as it does as a single interpolated sentence. It is presumably uttered by the speaker, not by the mushrooms, since it is not in quotation marks, but despite this it gives off a certain air of anonymity. It does not actually assert that the mushrooms are like the lost people, a simile which would tie it into its surrounding context; it is simply a brief, exclamatory utterance, possibly by the speaker or possibly not. The force of this is to prevent the poem from making too explicit an analogy between the mushrooms and the camp victims. The analogy is certainly implied; but to spell it out might risk robbing the mushrooms of their own specificity, reducing them to a mere symbol of something else. This might in turn imply that they deserved our sympathy only because they reminded us of the human condition, which would be unduly anthropocentric. The poem refuses to spell out the analogy, then, in order to preserve a tactful balance between attending to these fungi in their own right, and allowing a deeper human dimension to emerge obliquely from their plight.

The power of poetic form to rise above the materials with which it deals is also observable in this passage from Alexander Pope's mock-heroic poem *The Dunciad*, as the goddess Dullness ascends her throne to blot out reason and order from the world:

> Now flamed the dog-star's unpropitious ray,
> Smote every brain, and withered every bay;
> Sick was the sun, the owl forsook his bower,
> The moon-struck prophet felt the maddening hour:
> Then rose the seed of Chaos, and of Night,
> To blot out order and extinguish light,
> Of dull and venal a new world to mould,
> And bring Saturnian days of lead and gold.
> She mounts the throne: her head a cloud concealed,
> In broad effulgence all below revealed,

('Tis thus aspiring Dulness ever shines)
Soft on her lap her laureate son reclines.
Beneath her foot-stool, *Science* groans in chains,
And *Wit* dreads exile, penalties and pains.
There foamed rebellious *Logic*, gagged and bound,
There, stript, fair *Rhetoric* languished on the ground . . .

One might say that Pope's own riposte to this carnival of unreason is the literary form in which he portrays it. There is a balance and symmetry about these heroic couplets which reflect the reason, order and logic flouted by the apostles of Dullness. The couplet works by equipoise, antithesis and fine discrimination, whereas Dullness merges all distinctions into an amorphous sludge. Its polished trimness suggests an elegance beyond the reach of the poetic hacks whom Pope is lambasting here. Its clinching rhymes lend it an air of logic and precision, and the drastic economy of the form, distilling so much information in so brief a compass, demands the virtues of wit, exactness and lucidity. Each couplet forms a little enclosed world of relations and affinities, and as such becomes a microcosm of an orderly cosmos. The form of the poem itself, then, offers some resistance to the tedious long-windedness of those it is sending up.

4.4 Poetry and Performance

This kind of tension between form and content, of the kind we find in the mock-heroic of *The Dunciad*, is sometimes known to students of language as a performative contradiction. Roughly speaking, this means saying one thing while doing something which runs counter to it, like preaching the virtues of humility in a hectoring tone. In this sense, irony is a kind of performative contradiction. Male conference participants who rise to deliver lengthy, hotly indignant speeches about why no woman is contributing to the discussion, thus ensuring that no woman is able do so, are caught in such a bind. A performative contradiction is a useful concept because it reminds us that poems are performances, not simply objects on the page. We can think of a poem as a pattern of sound or meaning; but we can also see it as a strategy which aims to get something done. Or, indeed, a number of different, perhaps mutually incompatible things at the same time. To achieve this, the poem mobilises its army of formal devices; but this isn't to suggest that they always work harmoniously together. They may always pull in different directions.

There is, however, a paradox at stake here. Poetry is language organised in such a way as to generate certain effects, and to this extent it has much in common with everyday speech. One difference, as we have seen, is that everyday utterances usually skim over the flavour and texture of words in order to achieve their ends; whereas in poetry, one of these ends is precisely the exploration of words in themselves. This is how poetry can be rhetorical without being crudely instrumental. Part of the purpose for which it organises words is to reveal the nature of words. This, to be sure, is not its only function: it has a semantic dimension as well, which is to say that it is concerned with meaning as well as with investigating its own verbal materials. Or, as the aestheticians might say, the sign in poetry is at once communicative and autonomous. And though these two aspects of a poem do not always slide neatly together, as we shall see later, they have to be taken in terms of each other.

A poem, then, is a rhetorical performance, but (unlike most rhetorical exercises) not typically an instrumental one. It does things to us, though not usually so that we can get something done. Even so, there are forms of poetry which are written with the explicit intention of praising, cursing, consoling, inspiring, blessing, commemorating, denouncing, offering moral counsel and so on. Because the modern age is neurotically suspicious of the didactic, with its curious assumption that to be taught must be invariably unpleasant, it tends to imagine that poems which seek to do this must be inferior modes of writing. They are to be relegated to the lowly status of the pragmatic, along with bus tickets and 'No Entry' signs. But the didactic, a word which simply means 'teaching' and originally carried no pejorative overtones, is the purpose of one of the finest of all traditional literary genres, the sermon. Virgil's *Georgics*, as we have seen, includes technical advice to farmers (though they would be ill-advised to take it too seriously). Many an accomplished poem has been written with an immediate end in view. It is only the prejudice of the modern critic, for whom the practical is generally rather a vulgar affair, which obscures this fact. Some poems may be aesthetically poor but pragmatically rich, like the verses written by parents in memory of a dead child. Most modern critics revolt at the word 'dogma', too, but a great many traditional poems are dogmatic, in the original, non-derogatory sense of adhering to a system of belief. Dante and Milton, for example. It is a mistake to hold with some modern critics that too much belief, like too much salt, is invariably bad for you. It depends on the kind of belief in question. And the critics are of course usually thinking of other people's beliefs rather than their own. My beliefs are supremely flexible, while yours are absurdly arthritic.

Even so, poems are clearly not slices of propaganda. (This is another much-abused term, by the way: it originally meant simply the dissemination of information.) As W. H. Auden famously put the point:

> . . . For poetry makes nothing happen: it survives
> In the valley of its making where executives
> Would never want to tamper . . .
>
> ('In Memory of W. B. Yeats')

Yet this is only one side of the story. What poetry can make happen is a kind of constructive non-happening. By refraining from an immediate intervention in human affairs, it can allow truth and beauty to come about, in ways which may then make things happen.

The notion of strategy or performance reminds us that words have force as well as meaning. 'Force' means the effect or intended impact of a piece of language, which may not be at one with its meaning. What she actually said was 'It's getting awfully late', but the force of her statement was 'Why don't you leave this minute?' Poems do things to us as well as say things to us; they are social events as well as verbal artefacts. And the notion of a verbal event – of language as a practical activity – was known to the ancients as rhetoric, as we have seen already. Rhetoric means language organised in such a way as to achieve certain determinate ends, and this involves taking account of a whole number of considerations: the material nature of language itself; the way its various formal devices typically operate; the nature and capacities of its audience; and the social situation in which all this takes place. One modern term for this is 'discourse', which means language grasped as a concrete social occurrence inseparable from its context. It is language seen as a transaction between human subjects, rather than viewed formally or abstractly. All poetry has palpable designs on us, whatever John Keats may have considered. It is a matter of design in more senses than one. Poems are material events and fields of force, not simply verbal communications. Or rather, they are the latter only in terms of the former – which brings us once again to the question of form and content.

We can ask, then, what a piece of poetry is trying to do, as well as what it is trying to say. A relevant example might be the first two verses of T. S. Eliot's 'Mr Eliot's Sunday Morning Service':

> Polyphiloprogenitive
> The sapient sutlers of the Lord
> Drift across the window-panes.
> In the beginning was the Word.

In the beginning was the Word.
Superfetation of τò ἕν,
And at the mensual turn of time
Produced enervate Origen.

The reader's first response is one of blind panic. What on earth is going on here? Dutifully reaching for the dictionary proves only of limited help: we discover that 'sapient' means wise, or perhaps pretending to wisdom; that a sutler is someone who sells provisions to an army; that 'superfetation' means the fertilisation of the same ovum by different kinds of pollen, or a second conception during pregnancy which gives rise to embryos of different ages in the uterus. 'Polyphiloprogenitive' presumably means something like 'enjoying multiple reproduction'. (The dictionary will not help us here, just as it will not enlighten us as to why there is that curious full stop after the second 'In the beginning was the Word'.) 'Enervate' means deprived of vigour or vitality, which in this context (since Origen emasculated himself) may serve as a euphemism for 'castrated'. One scholar informs us that there is no such word as 'mensual', which may be a slip for 'menstrual', and that the Greek phrase contains a trifling error.[4] As we read on in the poem, the wild suspicion begins to dawn on us that the piece is actually about *bees*.

But none of this will get us very far. What we should have done was to trust our first impressions. This kind of writing is surely *meant* to baffle us. What it does is at least as important as what it says. Nobody fills a whole first line with the ridiculously tongue-twisting 'Polyphiloprogenitive' without some slyly mischievous intent. The esoteric diction and arcane allusions deliberately prevent us from reading for 'content'. Instead, we are held firmly at the level of the signifier, rammed helplessly up against its thickness and opacity. We are made to experience language itself, not what it points to. The language of the piece is so rebarbative, so bristling with pitfalls and enigmas, that we are forced to abandon trying to peer through it to the underlying meaning. And this, one imagines, is part of the effect which the poet is after. What the piece says, among other things, is 'This is modernism.' It proclaims itself as a type of literature which is impossible to consume. In fact, it represents a calculated guerrilla assault on the very idea of poetry. Or at least on the conception of poetry that the reader in 1920 might well have brought to these outrageously avant-garde verses.

Note, however, that the poem is not at all outrageous in metrical form. Instead, its metrical trimness leads us to expect a transparency of meaning

---

[4] See F. W. Bateson, 'The Poetry of Learning', in Graham Martin (ed.), *Eliot in Perspective* (London, 1970), p. 36.

which we are craftily denied by its language. And this metrical economy also lends it an impersonal air, one which allows it to get away to some extent with its shamelessly (or is it ironically?) self-flaunting display of erudition. It is a scandalously 'coterie' piece, accessible only to the cognoscenti; but because the poem's 'voice' seems purged of much distinctive personality, it is hard for us to feel that this is a matter of personal superiority. Eliot is often seen as an intellectually difficult, fearfully elitist writer, and so in some ways he was. But he was also the kind of poet who put little store by erudite allusions, and professed himself quite content to have his poetry read by those who had exceedingly little idea of what it meant. This should be deeply gratifying to us all. It was form – the material stuff of language itself, its archaic resonances and tentacular roots – which mattered most to him. In fact, he once claimed to have enjoyed reading Dante in the original even before he could understand Italian, which is perhaps pushing the centrality of poetic form a little too far.

This is one reason why the perversely misleading Notes to *The Waste Land* are largely spoof. In some ways, a semi-literate would have been Eliot's ideal reader. He was more of a primitivist than a sophisticate. He was interested in what a poem did, not what it said – in the resonance of the signifier, the lures of its music, the hauntings of its grains and textures, the subterranean workings of what one can only call the poem's unconscious. Eliot's poems are full of ghosts, even though his character Gerontion denies that he has any. Poetry sets up rhythms and resonances which in Eliot's view penetrate far beneath the intellect, infiltrating the visceral depths of the body and its secret psychical domains. It throws us the odd fragment of meaning, but only to keep us distracted while it goes to work upon us in stealthier, more devious ways.

The celebrated opening image of 'The Love-Song of J. Alfred Prufrock' is another case in point:

> Let us go then, you and I,
> When the evening is spread out against the sky
> Like a patient etherised upon a table . . .

The allusion to the evening and the sky sets up a conventionally Romantic expectation, which the following line casually or callously deflates. There is an equal baffling of expectations in the irregular rhythms of these three lines, which seem deliberately maladroit. The last two of them are rather dishevelled iambic pentameters. The lines lurch rather than glide, and the fact that the first two of them rhyme simply helps to throw their clumsily contrasting rhythms into relief. Their language is deliberately spiky and unlovely, more like the bleached bureaucratese of a form you might pick up in the post office than what we have come to expect from poetry.

How, the reader wonders, can the evening look like an anaesthetised body? Yet the point surely lies as much in the force of this bizarre image as in its meaning. We are in a modern world in which settled correspondences or traditional affinities between things have broken down. In the arbitrary flux of modern experience, the whole idea of representation – of one thing predictably standing for another – has been plunged into crisis; and this strikingly dislocated image, one which more or less ushers in 'modern' poetry with a rebellious flourish, is a symptom of this bleak condition. The point is not to ask how the evening can resemble an etherised patient, but what kind of alienated consciousness could make such an arbitrary, eccentric connection. It is a send-up of a simile.

It is the kind of question we might also ask about John Donne's 'Metaphysical' conceits, which are self-preening, virtuoso performances rather than plausible descriptions of reality. One of the most quoted passages in English poetry may demonstrate the point:

> Our two souls therefore, which are one,
>   Though I must go, endure not yet
> A breach, but an expansion,
>   Like gold to airy thinness beat.
>
> If they be two, they are two so
>   As stiff twin compasses are two;
> Thy soul, the fixed foot, makes no show
>   To move, but doth, if th'other do.
>
> And though it in the centre sit,
>   Yet when the other far doth roam,
> It leans and hearkens after it,
>   And grows erect, as that comes home.
>   ('A Valediction Forbidding Mourning')

We admire the appositeness of the compasses image at the same time as we feel the full force of its arbitrariness. If we did not sense the coerced nature of the conceit so keenly, the way it is wrenched wilfully into place by such perverse ingenuity, we would appreciate its skill a good deal less. What we watch is less the lovers than the sheer brio by which the poet manages to pull various ill-assorted bits and pieces of the world together, apparently against the odds. The poem tries to convince us that the lovers really are like a pair of compasses, at the same time as it rubs the disparity between them impudently in our faces and so persuades us into admiring its own deviously opportunistic wit.

Look, for another example, at the last two lines of George Herbert's poem 'Love', in which the poet is speaking to Christ:

> 'You must sit down', says Love, 'and taste my meat'.
> So I did sit and eat.

The sudden modulation in tone and metre here, from the formal courtesy of the first line to the quiet, throwaway matter-of-factness of the second, is a rhetorical effect. It is its impact on the reader which matters, not just its meaning. The full stop after 'meat' makes the last line a single unit, thus emphasising its terseness and flatness. A comma would have been fatal to the effect.

A much more abrupt transition than Herbert's can be found in T. S. Eliot's poem 'Burbank with a Baedeker: Bleistein with a Cigar':

> Princess Volupine extends
>   A meagre, blue-nailed, phthisic hand
> To climb the waterstair. Lights, lights,
>   She entertains Sir Ferdinand
>
> Klein. Who clipped the lion's wings
>   And flea'd his rump and pared his claws? . . .

'Klein', which means 'small' in German, is literally a comedown from the noble-sounding 'Sir Ferdinand', suggesting that this upstart Jew (Klein is also a Jewish surname) has been clipped of his bogus grandeur rather as the lion's wings are clipped. The poem actually performs a violent act of diminishing, even of humiliating, rather than simply speaking of it.

Or think of the opening lines of Book 2 of *Paradise Lost*, in which Milton introduces us to Satan on his kingly throne:

> High on a throne of royal state, which far
> Outshone the wealth of Ormus and of Ind,
> Or where the gorgeous East with richest hand
> Show'rs on her kings barbaric pearls and gold,
> Satan exalted sat . . .

The appearance of Satan is deferred to the fifth line, as with some florid introduction to a mighty personage which concludes by dramatically whisking back the curtain on him. The first four lines serve as a kind of flourish of trumpets to the devil's verbal entry into the poem. Presenting him amid this regal pomp makes it clear enough that Milton, a revolutionary republican, is definitely not of his party.

Or take the edgy exchange of challenges which opens *Hamlet*, as the sentry Francisco stands at his post on the castle battlements and his colleague Bernando arrives to relieve him:

Bernardo: Who's there?
Francisco: Nay, answer me. Stand and unfold yourself.

This terse snatch of dialogue is enough to tell us that nerves are not as steely as they might be in Hamlet's Elsinore. As scholars have pointed out, it is the soldier coming on sentry duty who barks out the traditional challenge, and the guard already on duty who responds. Francisco, his authority a mite flouted, presumably snarls 'Answer *me.*' We can detect the tonal emphasis from the social context. The force of the words, then, is distinct from their meaning; we cannot register it fully without some sense of context.

As far as the performative effects of poetry go, think also of Othello's grandiloquent first line as he comes marching on: 'Keep up your bright swords, for the dew will rust them.' This is, precisely, a grandiloquent first line, of the kind we imagine he might have been meticulously rehearsing for ten minutes in the wings. What the line says is 'Put away your swords', but its force is 'Here I am at last before your expectant gaze, the tragic hero with his rotund, dramatically arresting opening line.' It is almost as though the line, with its stately self-consciousness and sudden soaring of poetic temperature, is a quotation – in fact it caries a faint resonance of Christ in the Garden of Gethsemane. Othello, as usual, is performing himself magnificently – unlike Hamlet, who finds it hard to live up to himself, Macbeth, who performs himself as badly as a third-rate actor, and Lear, who hasn't a clue who he is.

The most renowned of all twentieth-century poems, T. S. Eliot's *The Waste Land*, betrays a different kind of discrepancy between form and content. The poem itself is a mighty collage of quotations, allusions, fractured phrases, spectral figures and listless snatches of memory. As such, it seems no more than a heap of fragments from a collapsed civilisation, of the kind that some archaeologist from the distant future might stumble across. Yet all this is being secretly woven, behind the reader's back, so to speak, into a dense tapestry of cross-references, symbols and archetypes, all of which holds at least some of these materials together. The result is an imposingly panoramic vision of decay and futility. But if such an authoritative overview is still possible, can civilisation really be all that fragmented after all?

Or to put it another way: how can the poem itself be possible, if what it says is true? Where does its structural unity spring from? Where is the poet himself standing?

4.5 Two American Examples

For a different illustration of this contrast, look at Robert Frost's much-loved 'Stopping by Woods on a Snowy Evening':

> Whose woods these are I think I know.
> His house is in the village though;
> He will not see me stopping here
> To watch his woods fill up with snow.
>
> My little horse must think it queer
> To stop without a farmhouse near
> Between the woods and frozen lake
> The darkest evening of the year.
>
> He gives his harness bell a shake
> To ask if there is some mistake.
> The only other sound's the sweep
> Of easy wind and downy flake.
>
> The woods are lovely, dark and deep,
> But I have promises to keep,
> And miles to go before I sleep,
> And miles to go before I sleep.

What is striking about these lines is the tension they set up between the everydayness of the event portrayed, which is reflected in the homespun, even quaint quality of the language, and the elaborate rhyme scheme which frames it. If the experience is about Nature, the intricate rhyming pattern, along with the odd well-honed phrase ('easy wind and downy flake') reminds us insistently that this is art. The event itself is low-key, while the closely packed rhymes thud as portentously as a heartbeat, made all the more obtrusive by the shortness of the lines.

The rhymes also stand out as they do because there is not much enjambement in the poem, which means, as we have seen, letting the sense run over from one line to another. When this happens, our eye tends to skim over the rhyme in its pursuit of the meaning from one line to the next. Here, however, many of the lines are units of meaning complete in themselves ('His house is in the village though' . . . 'The woods are lovely, dark and deep'), which allows us to savour the rhyming words to the full. The unvaried metre, with its regular, metronome-like tapping, contributes to this air of artifice; and all this is at odds with the naturalness of the content (the snow, woods and horse), and the sheer chanciness and spontaneity of the actual event. One might even describe this contrast as a kind of irony.

The rhyme scheme gives the appearance of moving forward only to keep curving back on itself: 'know', 'though', 'here', 'snow', 'queer', 'near', 'shake', 'mistake' and so on. We inch forward a shade only to find that we are also thrown back a pace or two. There is much recurrence and repetition in this *aaba / bbcb* rhyming pattern, which brings with it a curious sense of stasis. By the time the last verse arrives, we have the mesmeric, incantatory repetition of a single rhyme ('deep' . . . 'keep' . . . 'sleep'). There is no longer any progress or modulation in the rhyme scheme, even though the speaker is now reminding himself to move on. The effect is rather like someone trying to shake himself out of the paralysis of sleep with the thought that he should get up. Perhaps we can relate this sense of arrested motion to the death which we sense lurking in the shadow of these final lines. If death is part of what sleep and the woods symbolise, then the poem seems to find it both alluring and foreboding; and something similar can be said of its own rhyme scheme, which is beautifully managed yet also faintly ominous in its bell-like tolling. If the second 'And miles to go before I sleep' refers to the poet's death, then the fact that it is so distant should seem like a good thing; but the dying fall of the repetition make it sound more regrettable than reassuring. The poet has had a glimpse of a seductive stasis he is reluctant to abandon. It is a glimpse he has almost literally stolen from the owner of the woods, who, he assures himself rather guiltily, will not see him stopping here to take a look at his trees, rather as he would not see him furtively helping himself to some firewood.

This rather static form, which seems to revolve upon itself rather than move purposefully forward, thus reflects the suspended moment in the woods itself, where the poet's progress has been arbitrarily halted by the vision of the falling snow. The rhyme scheme moves in a kind of arrested motion, like a waterfall; and this is mirrored by the fact that what flickerings of life there are in the forest – the wind, the snow falling, the horse shaking its harness bells – are contained within a more general stillness. In this sense, form and content match one another as well as being at odds. It is as though the poem, like the speaker, is trying to forge ahead, but keeps being held back.

In another sense, however, form and content move at different levels. The poem's ritualised rhyming pattern, with its sober, almost fatalistic drumbeat, lends it a sense of inevitability; but there is nothing in the situation it depicts which would seem to warrant this. The situation itself is random, down-to-earth and open-ended, whereas the form is taut, closed and ceremonial. The horse shakes its bell to ask if there is some mistake – if stopping to watch the snow silently falling is a chance deviation from the regular course of events, which presumably it is. But the form of the poem could be seen as intimating otherwise. Its formal patterning, along with that reference to 'The darkest evening of the year', might be taken to hint that this fleeting experience in the woods is somehow 'meant' – that it is a kind of epiphany or revelation – at the same time as the language used to describe it suggests, quite to the contrary, that it is simply a natural, casual occurrence. The very fact that this is a poem, not an entry from a country diary, reinforces the sense of trembling on the brink of some obscure revelation. It is as though the form has a meaning which is at odds with the content. Perhaps the poet is being tempted to extract a meaning out of something which he suspects does not have one, and this is part of the poem's meaning. Perhaps all poetry is a sort of *trompe l'oeil* or illusion, plucking meaning out of materials which are senseless in themselves.

There is an unembellished, casually conversational feel to the poem's language, though the piece, ironically, is a monologue. The phrase 'fill up with snow', for example, is both delicately suggestive and entirely commonplace. So any too-obtrusive symbolism would risk overloading the verses. Perhaps this is one reason for the repetition in the last lines, which hints at a deeper, more 'metaphysical' meaning, but does so obliquely rather than explicitly. What the repetition does is to suddenly make the first 'And miles to go before I sleep', which we had taken literally, appear both literal and symbolic. It is as though the line has suddenly realised that it means more than it had imagined, and registers this by repeating itself. Poetry is not supposed to be just a bare record of experience; as we have seen, it is also expected to draw deeper or wider implications from what it observes. So perhaps Frost needs that final, portentous repetition, which implies in its muted way that the experience in the snow-filled woods points to more than itself.

In one sense, a repetition like this is a kind of clinching gambit, allowing us a sense of closure like the final, repeated chords of a classical symphony. Yet the closure is uneasy, since repetition can in principle go on forever, making the conclusion as open-ended in one sense as it is rounded off in another. Does the poem wrap itself up or simply trail off? Is the final line indeed a dying fall or exhausted murmur, or a slight turning up of volume and emotional intensity? The line wearily gets nothing new said; but saying nothing new may also suggest that there is nothing more to be said, thus giving the sense of an achieved conclusion.

This ominous intimation comes right at the end of the piece, which means that the poem cannot follow it up. In any case, we cannot be sure that it is an ominous gesture; it might just be a tired trailing off. If the poem prevents itself from pursuing its own intimation, however, given that it has just come to an end, it may be because of its respect for the integrity of the everyday world it describes. To move into a more visionary or metaphysical mode might risk undercutting its faith in ordinary things, a faith reflected in its idiomatic, scrupulously unshowy language. So the poem teeters on the brink of being 'symbolic', without quite taking the plunge. There is something elusive at the heart of this experience, yet the experience itself must not be devalued by being reduced to a mere symbol of whatever it is. Modern poets like Frost still want to make 'deep' statements; but they are also more sceptical of such high-sounding generalities than many of their forebears. So, rather like T. S. Eliot's *The Waste Land*, they gesture enigmatically to such profundities while at the same time being nervous of committing themselves to them. If this is true of the Frost poem, then the poem becomes to some extent an allegory of the dilemmas of modern poetry – which is to say, an allegory of itself.

There is another sense in which the poem might be seen as an allegory of poetry. The speaker is caught between continuing on his way in businesslike fashion, and staying put to relish the sight of the snow; and this represents a conflict between the pragmatic and the non-pragmatic. If the unpoetic, briskly commonsensical horse tugs him in one direction, the darkly mysterious woods draw him in another. Perhaps it is not surprising that Frost, who was both a poet and a farmer, should feel a tension between an aesthetic and an instrumental attitude to nature. The poem may be about how he would like simply to be a poet, savouring the sounds and textures of things, but can't afford to do so. So this prospect, like the prospect of death, is both seductive and unsettling. Looking too closely into things, exploring too adventurously beyond the familiar, may have its dangers, not least the danger of detaching you from the kind of common wisdom which the poem's language reflects. There may be something undemocratic about it. In the end, then, the poet throws in his lot with conventional morality ('But I have promises to keep') and the conservatively minded horse, who is a creature of habit as easily disturbed by innovation as the middlebrow reading public. But this option is not without it perils either. Anyway, Frost has produced a poem out of the tension between poetry and practicality, which should be enough for the present.

Contrast Frost's poem now with this one by Emily Dickinson:

> Because I could not stop for Death –
> He kindly stopped for me –
> The Carriage held but just Ourselves –
> And Immortality.
>
> We slowly drove – He knew no haste
> And I had put away
> My labor and my leisure too,
> For His Civility –
>
> We passed the School, where Children strove
> At Recess – in the Ring –
> We passed the Fields of Gazing Grain –
> We passed the Setting Sun –
>
> Or rather – He passed us –
> The Dews drew quivering and Chill –
> For only Gossamer, my Gown –
> My Tippet – only Tulle –
>
> We paused before a House that seemed
> A Swelling of the Ground –
> The Roof was scarcely visible –
> The Cornice – in the Ground –
>
> Since then – 'tis Centuries – and yet
> Feels shorter than the Day
> I first surmised the Horses' Heads
> Were toward Eternity –

The metre of this is more varied than in the Frost poem, as lines of four stresses alternate for the most part with lines of three. This gives the piece a more jaunty, less solemnly measured air than 'Stopping By Woods'. In fact, if you press this kind of rhythm far enough you end up with a sort of jingle. (It has been noted that almost all of Emily Dickinson's poems can be sung to the tune of 'The Yellow Rose of Texas'.) And this sprightliness is ironically at odds with those mournful, momentous allegorical figures of Death, Immortality and Eternity. The metre takes the sting out of these fearful abstractions, just as it does by setting them in as humdrum a context as a ride in a carriage. Yet the effect, far from being one of domesticating the unknown, is of a surreal strangeness, which the everyday imagery only sharpens. The whole scene is at once luminously etched and eerily unreal, as in a dream. As in some dreams, the speaker seems oddly unperturbed by the outlandish situation in which she finds herself. Somehow, the poem's very casualness about Death and Immortality – the sense that these figures are as familiar as old friends – adds to its uncanniness.

In this chapter, we have examined a number of poems in some detail, with particular attention to the way that form and content may work productively against one another. Part of the point of this exercise has been to challenge the piety that the two always form a harmonious whole. But there is an objection to the kind of close analysis we have been conducting, which we should tackle before we carry on.

Chapter 5

How to Read a Poem

5.1 Is Criticism Just Subjective?

There is an argument against the close analysis of literary form that goes something like this. Establishing what a poem literally says, or what metre it may use, or whether it rhymes, are objective matters on which critics can concur. (Punctuation also used to be ranked among these things, in the age before the owners of pubs began unwittingly casting doubt on the genuineness of their own products by advertising 'real' ale.) But talk of tone, mood, pace, dramatic gesture and the like is purely subjective. What I hear as rancorous you may hear as jubilant. You read as garrulous what strikes me as eloquent. Tone in a poem is not a matter of F major or B minor. Ironically, only a few features of form – metre and rhyme, for example – can actually be formalised. Form in poetry is mostly unformalisable. There can be no consensus on these questions, so it would be better to drop such fanciful talk altogether and concentrate on what we can be sure of.

There is something in this allegation. There is no exact science of these matters, and there is indeed a good deal of room for disagreement in discussing poems. But we may note to begin with that being able to disagree over an issue does not necessarily imply pure subjectivism. We might clash over whether torture is permissible or not, yet there may still be a right and wrong to the question, whatever our dissensions. We might disagree over whether someone is waving or drowning, but it is unlikely that he is doing both. Unless the swimmer has a remarkably nonchalant attitude to his death, one of us is almost bound to be wrong. Opinions we advance in purely conjectural style may later turn out to be cast-iron certainties, as more evidence becomes available.

As far as literary arguments go, take, for example, Robert Browning's darkly Gothic poem 'Porphyria's Lover', in which the speaker, possibly a psychopath, describes how he coolly decided to strangle his mistress:

> . . . I found
> A thing to do, and all her hair
> In one long yellow string I wound
> Three times her little throat around,
> And strangled her . . .
> And thus we sit together now,
> And all night long we have not stirred,
> And yet God has not said a word!

The offhandedness of that 'thing to do', as though the speaker might equally well have chosen to trim his moustache, is especially chilling. But how is one to read the last line? The most obvious interpretation is surely as a cry of (perhaps slightly manic) triumph: the lover has deliberately tempted God by this dreadful deed into revealing himself, and God has remained silent. So perhaps the whole grisly murder was an experiment in demonstrating the truth of atheism. Yet I have heard the line delivered by an actor in a tone of sullen resentment. For this reader, no doubt, the speaker is not a jubilant atheist but a would-be believer, who has sacrificed his lover in an attempt to force God into revealing his hand, and is now bitterly downcast by the Almighty's obdurate silence. He has, so to speak, lost his Maker and his mistress at the same time, and all for nothing.

There is no foolproof way of deciding between such competing interpretations. We cannot appeal to Browning, and even if we could it might well not settle the question. This is not only because poets can be peculiarly obtuse about the meaning of their own work. T. S. Eliot, for example, once described *The Waste Land* as just a kind of rhythmic grousing, though he was probably being disingenuous. It is also because when Browning was once asked what one of his poems meant, he replied that at the time of writing it, 'God and Robert Browning knew; now, God knows.' Yet those who feel that these questions are too chancy and subjective, in contrast with 'what the poem says', might care to note that 'what the poem says' is not always that well-founded either. Take, for example, Browning's title. We know that Porphyria is the name of the murdered woman, since the poem makes this clear. Which means that the lover must be the male speaker. But why do we assume that the speaker is male? There is nothing in the text to indicate this. It is simply a hypothesis we bring to the piece in order to make sense of it. Perhaps the speaker is also a woman, and this is a lesbian relationship gone horribly awry.

No doubt it would be rather brazen to adduce the phrase 'tonight's gay feast' in support of this hypothesis. It is also the case that the vast majority of murderers are men, not least those killers driven by sadistic sexual motives. The arrogant sexual possessiveness of the speaker is much more stereotypically masculine than feminine. And the odds against an eminent Victorian poet writing a piece about lesbian sexuality, however cunningly he concealed it, are positively astronomical. Titles are part of poems, and we may note that this title, significantly, refers to the murderer and not his victim. So even the title reflects a morbid self-obsession which, stereotypically speaking, is arguably more masculine than feminine. (Actually, one suspects that Browning put the lover rather than the victim in the title to place some distance between himself and his protagonist, treating him as a pathological case.) Even so, we cannot absolutely rule out a lesbian reading. One of the apparently most self-evident facts about the poem turns out to be contestable.

Questions of tone crop up again in these celebrated lines from Andrew Marvell's 'To His Coy Mistress':

> But at my back I always hear
> Time's wingèd chariot hurrying near:
> And yonder all before us lie
> Deserts of vast eternity.
> Thy beauty shall no more be found;
> Nor, in thy marble vault, shall sound
> My echoing song: then worms shall try
> That long-preserved virginity,
> And turn your quaint honour to dust,
> And into ashes all my lust.
> The grave's a fine and private place,
> But none, I think, do there embrace.

As with a lot of so-called Metaphysical poetry, the speaker seems sportive and serious at the same time, so that a good actor delivering these lines would need to convey their urbane sophistry (the speaker is really just trying to get her into bed with a lot of high-toned metaphysics), along with their undertow of urgency and anxiety (he really is worried about decay and death). It is possible that he is being both debonair and deadly earnest, and to suppose this makes the piece more interesting and ambiguous. The tone of the last two lines, depending on how you judge the overall ratio between erotic teasing and ontological anxiety, could be anything from roguish to playfully sardonic to cuttingly sarcastic. You could deliver them to reveal a real impatience and irascibility beginning to peep through the cavalier wit, or as impishly bantering, or as a piece of hard-boiled flippancy.

Tone, mood and the like may be matters of interpretation over which critics can conflict; but this is not the same as their being purely subjective. As we have just seen, we can conflict over meaning as well. But there are usually limits to such contentions. It is just possible that Porphyria's lover is a woman, in the sense that you can adopt this hypothesis and still make sense of the work; but nobody would suggest that the lover is a giraffe. This is not just because Victorian writers did not generally go in for poems about bestiality, but because the textual evidence simply would not support it. Giraffes do not wind people's hair three times around their throat and strangle them. Their hearts do not swell at the thought that they are worshipped by a woman. Nor do they entertain thoughts about God, atheistic or otherwise. If someone asked us how we know that giraffes do not spend their time feverishly brooding on metaphysical questions, it would be enough to reply: by looking at what they do. We do not have to get inside their brains to be reasonably sure of this, just as I do not have to get inside your brain to know that when I see you rolling at my feet with your hair on fire emitting strange noises, you are clearly not happy.

Something of the same is true of more elusive questions like mood, address, implication, connotation, symbolism, sensibility, rhetorical effect and the like. There can be serious divergences of opinion about these things, but there are also constraints on how deeply these may run, at least for those who share the same culture. This is because tones and feelings are quite as much social matters as meaning. It is not that meaning is public whereas feeling is private. It is only a disreputable philosophical tradition which persuades us to think this way. On this theory, my feelings are something private and subjective. I know them inwardly, intuitively, simply by looking inside myself. But if this is so, it is hard to see how I can ever misidentify what I am feeling. It becomes difficult to say things like 'I don't know whether I'm afraid of her or not', or 'I thought at the time that I cared for him, but looking back I realise that I didn't care for him in the least.' In any case, when I look into myself, how do I identify what I find there? How do I know that what I am feeling is envy and not disgust? Only because I already have the concept of envy to help me identify this feeling among the whole welter of emotions and sensations I discover when I reflect on myself. And I learnt this concept by being introduced into a language as a child. If I did not have language I would still have feelings, but I would not know what they were. And some feelings which I have now I would not have at all.

Bertolt Brecht puts the point well:

> One easily forgets that human education proceeds along highly theatrical lines. In a quite theatrical manner the child is taught how to behave; logical arguments only come later. When such-and-such occurs, it is told (or sees), one must laugh. It joins in when there is laughter, without knowing why; if asked why it is laughing it is wholly confused. In the same way it joins in shedding tears, not only weeping because the grown-ups do so but also feeling genuine sorrow. This can be seen at funerals, whose meaning escapes children entirely. These are theatrical events which form the character. The human being copies gestures, miming, tones of voice. And weeping arises from sorrow, but sorrow also arises from weeping.[1]

Brecht's case is rather too 'culturalist': very small babies laugh, for example, long before they have grasped the social institution of laughter. They also cry and smile, activities which have a biological basis. Even so, Brecht is on to something vitally important, which he has learnt not 'philosophically' but through his practical activity as a playwright and theatre director. Emotion in the theatre is clearly a public affair, which is not so obviously the case in the bedroom. Brecht spent much of his life watching actors *learn* modes of feeling, and the kinds of speech and behaviour which seemed appropriate to them. The theatre could show him something about real life which real life tended to conceal. He was able to extend what he found in theatre rehearsals to human emotions in general, and their 'mimetic' or imitative character. Being brought up in a culture is a matter of learning appropriate forms of feeling as much as particular ways of thinking. And all of these are sedimented in that culture's language and behaviour, so that to share a language is to share a form of life. To imagine that this means that our feelings are never sincere would be like thinking that I can never use the words 'I love you' and mean them because millions of people have used them before.

In a culture which lacked the concept and institution of private property, for example, one could not conceive a burning desire to become a billionaire entrepreneur. This is not to claim that such a culture would be without feelings of greed or ambition, simply without these specific forms of them. People do not generally feel revolted by the very sight of their second cousin if they do not inhabit cultures in which there are strong taboos on their marrying them. What we can feel is to some extent determined by the kinds of

[1] *Brecht on Theatre: The Development of an Aesthetic* (London, 1964), p. 152. See also Terry Eagleton, 'Brecht and Rhetoric' in Eagleton, *Against the Grain: Essays 1975–1985* (London, 1986).

material animals we are. But what we might call styles of feeling are shaped by our cultural institutions. And both of these are public affairs.

Children, then, observe various kinds of behaviour around them, and learn to grasp this as *expressive* behaviour. Their understanding of emotions is thus bound up with the kind of material things people do, and with their own growing participation in such practical forms of life. Like actors (though not, in fact, Brechtian actors), they sometimes begin by miming styles of emotion and end up by feeling them for real. In cultures like our own, they then usually go on to be taught that feelings are private, natural, internal and universal. But this is just how our kind of culture feels about feelings. There are indeed natural, universal feelings, such as grief at the death of a loved one, which we have because we are the kind of creatures we are; but what we make of that grief is a cultural affair. And there are other emotions, such as feeling embarrassed about using the wrong cutlery at a formal dinner party, which might be unintelligible to some other cultures.

It is also hard to see why we should think of our emotions as being 'inside' us, and so shut off from public view. It seems strange to say of someone who is busy smashing up the furniture and tearing out great clumps of his hair that his anger is inside him. We can conceal or dissemble our emotions, of course, but they are not hidden by nature; and concealing them is a complex social practice which we have to learn. Infants, unfortunately, have not yet got the hang of it. One sees what it means to say that someone who is behaving maliciously has malice 'inside' her, since malice is among other things a matter of feelings, and feelings are not part of the public world in the same way that pool tables are. In another sense, however, to say this is as odd as to say that someone who is singing has the notes inside her. It is simply a misleading way of saying that it is *she* who is singing or feeling malice, not someone else. Emotions are not private affairs which we can occasionally choose to put on display, not even for the English. This is as false as the idea that meaning is a private process in our heads.

An example of a falsely subjective approach to feeling can be found in the singer Van Morrison's versions of some Irish songs. What is amiss with Morrison's performances, at least for some of us devotees of traditional Irish music, is that they seem to regard emotion as something to be superadded to the tunes and lyrics. This is why Morrison engages in so much florid, 'feelingful' improvisation when singing them, inserting a wailing repetition here or a choked bit of sobbing there. It is as though he does not trust his material enough to appreciate that the feelings are, so to speak, already *there* in the songs, inseparable from their words and music. The tunes and lyrics are as they are because they express or embody certain patterns of feeling in their actual materials; so that if these materials were different, the emotional patterns would be different too. Listening to Morrison, one is tempted to adapt a line by Wallace Stevens about another singer: 'But it was he and not the song we heard.'

It is as if Morrison's performances in this field reflect a flawed epistemology, surprised though he would doubtless be to hear it. If only he would stop indulging in sudden snatches of 'passion' and heartfelt heavy breathing, he might come to see that he does not need to add his own 'subjective' feelings to the songs. All he has to do, like a *sean-nós* (traditional) Irish singer, is to articulate them by letting them flow through him, rather than to stamp his 'personality' all over them. Such an articulation is 'subjective' in the sense that every singer or musician does things in his or her own way; but it is not 'subjective' in the sense that the meaning and emotional power of these pieces are purely in the gift of the performer. This is one reason why Irish musicians have been known to perform with their backs to the audience.

To regard feeling as subjectively superadded is also to see the songs themselves as so much inert material waiting for life to be breathed into them by the performer. The other side of subjectivism is objectivism. The songs are just brutely there, senseless and emotionless in themselves, to be stirred into expressive meaning at the touch of a human subject. It is a view which subtly devalues everything but human consciousness, and is thus, for all its pious cult of feeling, a typical piece of humanistic arrogance.

5.2   Meaning and Subjectivity

Just the same view can be taken of language. For one kind of theorist, poems are just meaningless black marks on a page, and it is the reader who constructs them into sense. This is true in one sense and false in another. We may note first of all that to speak of 'meaningless black marks' already involves us in meanings. It is notoriously hard to get back behind meaning altogether, for much the same reasons as it is impossible to imagine ourselves dead. We may also note that to regard words as black marks is an abstraction from what we actually see on a page. And this is an operation which already requires a good deal of interpretative labour. Every now and then, we see a row of black marks and then realise that what we are seeing is words, just as every now and then we see a large grey patch and then realise that we are looking at an elephant. Most of the time, however, we see words and elephants, not black marks and grey patches. Someone who keeps seeing grey patches where he ought to be seeing elephants should pay a visit either to his optician or his psychiatrist.

It is true, even so, that all we literally have are words on a page. Reading these words as a poem means restoring to them something of their lost material body. It involves grasping them as tonal, rhythmical, metrical, emotional, intentional, expressive of meaning, and so on. In a face-to-face dialogue, the material body of language is as solidly present as its meanings are, and this acts as a control on interpretation. We know that the tone is despairing because the other person is clutching a sodden handkerchief and tottering on a very high window ledge. Or we can ask a speaker whether he is being sarcastic, and adjust our understanding of his words accordingly. Or we know that she does not intend 'Let us put continents between us!' metaphorically because she is handing us our air ticket to Sydney as she speaks. Poetry is language which comes without these contextual clues, and which therefore has to be reconstructed by the reader in the light of a context which will make sense of it. And such contexts are in embarrassingly plentiful supply. Yet they are not just arbitrary either: on the contrary, they are shaped in turn by the cultural contexts by which the reader makes sense of the world in general.

So in one sense none of the formal features we have been examining is actually 'there' on the page. But neither are they just arbitrarily implanted by the reader. If this were so, then the reader could make a particular pattern of black marks mean anything she chose, which would be to strip her of her culture. Belonging to a culture means that not everything is up for grabs all of the time, as it might be for a cultureless being like God. It means that the world comes to us not as brute fact or raw material, but as already signifying. And this applies as much to the words on a page as to a *coup d'état* or a telegraph pole. Being part of a culture also entails that we are not inexorably bound by these built-in interpretations, as we can imagine a crocodile being constrained by its biology to interpret certain kinds of stuff as edible. Some cultural versions of the world (the assumption that eating boot polish is excellent for your health, for example) are fairly free-floating, and thus quite easy not to be coerced by. But because a lot of interpretations are actually built in to our form of life, resisting them (if that seems the right thing to do) involves us in a struggle. And there are some solidly entrenched assumptions and investments built into our culture which we probably could not even imagine being without, like the assumption that there are other people.

We can make the cluster of black marks 'syrup' mean 'historicism', given enough context. But we cannot do it just by deciding to do it, since this would be a meaningless ceremony. We would not be able to make the new meaning stick. It would simply have no force within our social life. Since meanings are deeply bound up with our cultural behaviour, we cannot change language radically without transforming a lot of what we actually get up to. To think otherwise, to adopt an image of Wittgenstein's, would be like a man passing money from one of his hands to the other and thinking that he had made a financial transaction.[2] All the same, one could imagine a situation in which 'syrup' plausibly meant 'historicism'. Perhaps the more traditionalist members of an English department wish to conceal their contempt for historicism from their more avant-garde colleagues, and adopt this code in order to do so. But doing this means being aware of what 'syrup' commonly means, or at least being aware that it is not commonly regarded as a synonym for 'historicism'. Opting for a new meaning involves being conscious of the culturally agreed one. In any case, one could not even have the concept of 'new meaning' unless one already had a language.

Take, for example, the question of connotation. It is characteristic of poetic language that it gives us not simply the denotation of a word (what it refers to), but a whole cluster of connotations or associated meanings. It differs in this respect from legal or scientific language, which seeks to pare away surplus connotations in the name of rigorous denotation. By and large, legal and scientific language aims to constrict meaning, whereas poetic language seeks to proliferate it. This is not a value judgement: there are times when the rigorous definition of a word is just what we need (it may come in handy, for example, when we are up in court on a treason charge), and there are other times when it is pleasant to cut the signifier free from its anchorage in a single sense and let it interbreed with other bits of sense.

Connotations are less controllable than denotations, which is one reason why lawyers, scientists and bureaucrats are nervous of them. But doesn't this then pose a problem for poets? If connotation is a kind of free associating, how can a poem ever come to mean anything definite? What if Shakespeare's line 'Shall I compare thee to a summer's day?' reminds me irresistibly of fried bananas? The brief answer to this is that meaning is not a matter of psychological associations. Indeed, there is a sense in which it is not a 'psychological' matter at all. Meaning is not an arbitrary process in our heads, but a rule-governed social practice; and unless the line 'Shall I compare thee to a summer's day?' could plausibly, in principle, suggest fried bananas to other readers as well, it cannot be part of its meaning.

It may be that Shakespeare's Cordelia reminds me of a cross-dressed version of my uncle Arthur; but I am aware that this is not the case for those

---

[2] All references in this work to Wittgenstein are taken from his *Philosophical Investigations* (Oxford, 1953).

readers who have not had the pleasure of meeting my uncle Arthur; and that Shakespeare, for all his prescience and preternatural insight, was unlikely to have had my uncle Arthur in mind when he wrote *King Lear*. There are, to be sure, all kinds of situations in which the line between the private and public connotations of words is uncertain. But unless a connotation can plausibly exist for someone else, it cannot exist as a meaning for me either. The stray personal associations which drift in and out of our heads when we are reading *Lear* are of interest to our psychotherapist, not to the literary critic. Meaning is not a matter of having pictures in your head. You can enjoy Blake or Rilke with no pictures in your head at all.

So meanings are neither randomly bestowed by readers, nor objectively there on the page in the sense that a watermark is. The same goes for value judgements. Value judgements are not objective in the sense that mahogany cocktail cabinets are, but this does not mean that they are simply a matter of private whim. In any culture, there are certain complex sets of criteria as to what counts as good or bad poetry; and although there can be an enormous amount of disagreement over how these criteria are to be applied, or whether they are valid in the first place, their application is far from just a subjective affair. People may wrangle over whether a particular patch of colour counts as green, but this does not mean that 'green' is a purely subjective judgement. It is possible to see that a poem is a fine achievement yet dislike it intensely, just as you can love a poem you regard as aesthetically atrocious; and this suggests that value judgements are not the same as private tastes. 'I do like a good bad poem' is not an unintelligible statement. Much the same goes for such matters as mood, register, pitch, pause, and so on, upon which overall value judgements are built. If these are not just arbitrary, it is partly because they are so closely bound up with meaning, and meaning is not something that we simply legislate. A poem does not instruct us that it is meant to be melancholic; but this mood, even so, may be in some sense built into its language.

Take, as an illustration of melancholy, the first verse of Tennyson's poem 'Mariana':

> With blackest moss the flower-plots
>   Were thickly crusted, one and all:
> The rusted nails fell from the knots
>   That held the pear to the gable-wall.
> The broken sheds looked sad and strange:
>   Unlifted was the clinking latch;
>   Weeded and worn the ancient thatch

> Upon the lonely moated grange.
> She only said, 'My life is dreary,
> He cometh not,' she said.
> She said, 'I am aweary, aweary,
> I would that I were dead!'

There is nothing in principle to stop us from reading this aloud as though it were intended to be uproariously funny, gasping with giggles and chortling uncontrollably. Many a high-toned poem from the past seems hilarious to us in the present. But we do not usually assume that these works were *intended* to be hilarious. There is something mildly comic about the iron predictability of the word 'dead' in the last line of this stanza, but the effect is clearly unwitting. There is no obvious signal that the poem is sadistically sending up its protagonist, winking roguishly at us over her head at the sight of her dejection. How do we know that the mood of this verse is supposed to be gloomy? It would be enough to say that we spoke English. Words and phrasings like 'I am aweary, aweary, / I would that I were dead!' have a certain kind of sensibility or emotional value built into them. People do not tend to say this sort of thing when they have just been bequeathed a fine old Tudor farmhouse along with several thousand acres of fertile land.

What is amiss with the piece, in fact, is that it is all too obvious what mood it intends to nurture. The emotional climate of the piece is far too coherent. Almost every word, sound and image is remorselessly dragooned into the overall atmospheric effect, in an absurdly homogenising way. A useful adjective to describe this is *voulu*, which means 'willed' in French and which suggests too contrived, self-conscious an effort. The piece lacks the faintest flicker of spontaneity. Nothing in this windless enclosure is allowed to have a life of its own, or to kick back against the stifling climate of woe in which it is shrouded. Even the nails fall obediently from the wall, dutifully performing their minor role in the whole over-orchestrated scene.

The piece is meticulously overwrought. Despite its technical adeptness, it succeeds only in being inert about inertia. It is thus an illustration of what is sometimes called the mimetic fallacy, whereby poets try to justify the fact that their works are dishevelled or unbelievably boring by claiming that messiness or boredom is what they are about. Even the rhyme scheme is pressed into the service of this stagnant oppressiveness, with that 'strange' / 'latch' / 'thatch' / 'grange' pattern in the middle lines. This *abba* style of rhyming, which Tennyson also puts to work in his most celebrated poem 'In Memoriam', has a curiously haunting, plangent effect, as well as creating a sense of revolving solemnly in a circle. It is a suitable sort of rhyme for a poem in which the heroine's existence has been frozen into a single, sluggish moment of time.

It is not for us, then, just to decide on what mood is at stake here. In a similar way, it is not just up to us to determine what sort of feeling someone's behaviour is expressing. We have noted already that people may dissemble their feelings, but this is not to deny that there is an internal relation between what they feel and what they do. If there were not, they would not need to dissemble. Besides, poets, like goldfish, are incapable of dissembling. This is not because they are searingly honest, but because whether authors of fiction really did experience an emotion they write about is not the point. As we have seen, the word 'fiction' cues us not to ask such irrelevant questions. We can ask whether a piece of poetry sounds sincere or insincere, but we cannot determine this by finding out whether the poet actually had the experience she is portraying. The author may have done so and still sound insincere. The fact that you really have been abducted by aliens on numerous occasions does not automatically make your account of it convincing. Shakespeare did not need to experience sexual jealousy in order to create Othello. When he penned some of Hamlet's most magnificently distraught speeches, perhaps all he was feeling was whether the imagery sounded suitably diseased.

Sincerity and insincerity in poetry are qualities of language, not (at least for literary critics) moral virtues. In his embarrassing poem 'Chicago', Carl Sandburg praises the city in these terms:

Come and show me another city with lifted head singing so proud to be alive
    and coarse and strong and cunning.
Flinging magnetic curses amid the toil of piling job on job, here is a tall bold
    slugger set vivid against the little soft cities;
Fierce as a dog with tongue lapping for action, cunning as a savage pitted against
    the wilderness . . .

Sandburg may genuinely have had these feelings, but the slapdash language (*magnetic* curses?), limply stereotypical phrases ('cunning as a savage') and macho swagger suggest that the feelings themselves are bogus. We cannot establish whether a piece of language is sincere simply by consulting the speaker or writer. Someone may imagine that they are deriving a mystical experience from an appalling bit of doggerel, but they must surely be mistaken. They may be having a profound experience for some other reason (perhaps they are sipping vintage claret while they are reading, or thrusting red-hot needles into an effigy of Donald Trump), but the poem itself could not be the reason for their emotion. A poem can be the *occasion* for an emotion, as when those who are grieving the loss of a child find comfort in some lushly sentimental verses. But 'literary' feelings are *responses* to poems, not just states of emotion which occur in their presence. And for a feeling to count as a response, there must be some internal relation between it and the poem itself.

Our actions are expressive of feelings in the same way that words are expressive of meanings. There can be all sorts of ambiguities about what someone is feeling, just as there can be about what they are meaning. We speak of the feeling 'behind' someone's actions, just as we speak of the meaning 'behind' someone's words; but this spatial metaphor is surely misleading. When Cleopatra says that she wore Mark Antony's sword, the fact that her meaning is unclear (does she mean this literally, or is it sexual symbolism?) is not because it lies 'behind' her words, as though it is too remote to gain access to. This would be like thinking that not being certain whether a painting is of a storm at sea or the wild white locks of an elderly lunatic is because its subject matter lies 'behind' the painted shapes on the canvas. When someone is cowering and gibbering with fear, their fear is present in their bodily activity in the same way that a meaning is present in a word. But this does not mean that we could not misinterpret their fear as rage or shame.

5.3   Tone, Mood and Pitch

So we can misinterpret, say, the tone of a poem. But this is not because the tone lies 'behind' the words, or because the reader arbitrarily assigns a tone to words which are toneless in themselves. Let us look, for example, at the final stanza of W. B. Yeats's 'A Dialogue of Self and Soul':

> I am content to follow to its source
> Every event in action or in thought;
> Measure the lot; forgive myself the lot!
> When such as I cast out remorse
> So great a sweetness flows into the breast
> We must laugh and we must sing,
> We are blest by everything,
> Everything we look upon is blest.

Most readers will hear a defiantly exultant tone here, though some may also discern a touch of bravado and some may not. It might be thought that 'Measure the lot; forgive myself the lot!' is rather too self-satisfied a gesture, with just a hint of virile bluster; but some may simply hear it as a rather agreeable kind of gusto. Some readers may query that phrase 'When such as I . . .', which might be taken to insinuate that especially momentous consequences will flow from the poet's casting out of remorse since he is a good deal more morally conscientious than the average run of folk. In fact, the grammar of the lines that follow, with the shift of preposition from 'I' to 'we', implies that the speaker's act of self-acceptance has a transfigurative effect not just upon himself but on everyone else as well. He has managed to relieve not only his own guilt but that of the whole human race, an achievement previously regarded as confined to Jesus Christ.

Yet there is also something moving, as often with Yeats, about the bold, apparently artless directness of the lines and their jubilant, chant-like refrain ('We must laugh and we must sing, / We are blest by everything'). It is though the lines risk a certain naivety, trusting as they do to a deeper wisdom. 'So great a sweetness flows into the breast' could only be a line by Yeats, with its boldly self-assured stress on a single, simple word ('sweetness') rather than some more complex term or phrase. Whereas Keats goes in for compound epithets like 'cool-rooted', Yeats tends to prefer simple, elemental words like 'great', 'beat', 'stone', 'fool', 'bread', 'trod', 'glitter'. 'Sweet' and 'sweetness' figure among these. If he wants to suggest human squalor he writes something like 'foul ditch'; and these stock words and phrases, used recurrently, come to assume the status of a kind of code, accruing complex meanings which do not need to be spelled out but which seem communicable at a glance. Yeats has a most unmodernist faith in his verbal medium, one inherited in part from the Irish oral tradition. He does not appear to feel that words need to be skewed, telescoped or overpacked in order to have an effect. If something in his poetry is ambiguous, it is probably a mistake.

'Everything we look upon is blest' is a questionable enough claim, but the reader probably lets Yeats get away with it since his ecstatic triumph, seen in the context of the poem as a whole, seems dearly enough won. He has paid for it in bitter experience, rather than bought it on the cheap. Compare those lines, then, with these from his poem 'The Tower':

> And I declare my faith:
> I mock Plotinus' thought
> And cry in Plato's teeth,
> Death and life were not
> Till man made up the whole,
> Made lock, stock and barrel
> Out of his bitter soul,
> Aye, sun and moon and star, all,
> And further add to that

> That, being dead, we rise,
> Dream and so create
> Translunar Paradise. . . .

If the first passage is a matter of defiant exultation, this, surely, is one of pompous self-indulgence. The booming, bombastic tone, which seems to hold the lines together by sheer bull-headed assertion, is of a piece with the doctrinal arrogance of 'Death and life were not / Till man made up the whole'. The fact that this statement is palpably untrue does nothing to intensify its poetic force. Something seems to have gone momentarily awry with the iambic trimeter in that line 'Aye, sun and moon and star, all', which compels us to gabble 'sun and moon and star' if we are to keep the stresses regular, while 'And further add to that' sounds more like a solicitor dictating to his secretary than a sage about to divulge a mystical secret. The terseness of the lines is perhaps meant to have a vatic effect, but come through as merely sententious. 'Translunar Paradise' is not made any less bogus or unbelievable by those thrustingly assertive capital letters. There are, however, some strikingly inventive para-rhymes: 'faith' / 'teeth', 'thought' / 'were not', 'that' / 'create' and (much less felicitously) 'barrel' / 'star, all'.

Tone means a modulation of the voice expressing a particular mood or feeling. It is one of the places where signs and emotions intersect. So tones can be arch, abrupt, dandyish, lugubrious, rakish, obsequious, urbane, exhilarated, imperious and so on. But it is not easy to distinguish tone in poetry from mood, which the dictionary defines as a state of mind or feeling. Perhaps we could say that the mood of 'Mariana' is melancholic, while the tone is doleful or lugubrious. Then there is timbre, which means the distinctive character of a voice or musical note, apart from its pitch and intensity. Timbre in the Tennyson piece could be taken to denote its uniquely Tennysonian quality, one that would be unmistakable to anyone who has read a fair amount of his poetry. We are speaking here of a poet's distinctive hallmark or signature. Robert Lowell's verses are very Lowellish, while nothing is more Plath-like than a Sylvia Plath poem. Swinburne, alas, never ceases to be Swinburnian.

We can speak, too, of the pitch of a poetic voice, meaning whether it sounds high, low or middle-ranging. One might imagine the pitch of the last line of 'Porphyria's Lover' – 'And yet God has not said a word!' – as either a high-spirited whoop or a low growl, depending on how one interprets its meaning. Like most other aspect of form, pitch is bound up with what sense we make of the words. One can even talk of a poem's volume, meaning how loud or soft it sounds. Nobody could read these lines of George Herbert as a hushed whisper:

> I struck the board and cried, 'No more;
> I will abroad!
> What? Shall I ever sigh and pine?
> My lines and life are free, free as the road,
> Loose as the wind, as large as store.
> Shall I be still in suit?'
>
> ('The Collar')

We know that the poet is shouting here because he tells us so. We can feel his anger and frustration in the abrupt, quick-fire shifts of rhythm, the helplessly broken phrases, the way the lines deliberately fail to cohere into a shapely semantic pattern despite their graphological shapeliness on the page. Similarly, John Donne's line 'For God's sake hold your tongue, and let me love', with its air of jocular impatience, is presumably not meant to be delivered in a blandly self-effacing voice. Nor is this feminist clarion call from Anna Laetitia Barbauld:

> Yes, injured Woman! rise, assert thy right!
> Woman! too long degraded, scorned, oppressed;
> O born to rule in partial Law's despite,
> Resume thy native empire o'er the breast!
>
> ('The Rights of Woman')

Barbauld overdoes the exclamation marks, but there is no other piece of punctuation designed to stress a rise of volume or intensity. They are the most expressive of punctuation marks, if also the most unsubtle.

Some poems, however, are so deathly quiet that we have to strain our ears to catch what they are saying. Another piece of Tennyson, this time from 'In Memoriam', may serve as an example:

> Be near me when my light is low,
> When the blood creeps, and the nerves prick
> And tingle; and the heart is sick,
> And all the wheels of Being slow . . .
>
> Be near me when I fade away,
> To point the term of human strife,
> And on the low dark verge of life
> The twilight of eternal day.

This sounds rather like the hoarse, whispered words of a terminally ill patient, so that we have to lean in close to the pillow to hear what is being murmured. It would be incongruous to deliver it in a raucous bellow, as it wouldn't be to bawl out the immortal opening lines of Tennyson's 'Charge of the Light Brigade': 'Half a league, half a league, / Half a league onward . . .'. How do we know this? We pick it up as we pick up the fact that twilight comes at the end of the day. It is part of our cultural behaviour.

5.4   Intensity and Pace

Intensity is another category of poetic feeling, distinct from tone, pitch and volume. There are muted intensities as well as full-blooded ones. This extract from a sonnet by Elizabeth Barrett Browning could not be read as flippant:

> How do I love thee? Let me count the ways.
> I love thee to the depth and breadth and height
> My soul can reach, when feeling out of sight
> For the ends of Being and ideal Grace.
> I love thee to the level of every day's
> Most quiet need, by sun and candlelight.
> I love thee freely, as men strive for Right.
> I love thee purely, as they turn from Praise . . .

This is too earnest and high-minded for modern taste. 'For the ends of Being and ideal Grace' is gauche and too much of a mouthful, while 'to the level of' sounds an oddly prosaic note. We also tend to be put off by weighty capitalised abstractions like 'Right' and 'Praise'. But the Victorians would presumably not have found the poem excessively intense. The poem uses the rhyme form Milton tended to favour in his sonnets, one which in the first eight lines (or octave) employs an *abba* scheme twice. This is also typical of Petrarch's sonnets. Another Victorian woman, Christina Rossetti, handles this double *abba* rhyme scheme more adroitly:

> Remember me when I am gone away,
> Gone far away into that silent land;
> When you can no more hold me by the hand,
> Nor I half turn to go yet turning stay.
> Remember me when no more day by day
> You tell me of our future that you planned:
> Only remember me; you understand
> It will be late to counsel then or pray . . .

The rhymes here, tolling like a bell, are vital to the mournful mood. As often in Victorian verse, the *abba* is emphasised graphically as well, by indenting the two middle lines. Some readers may find Rossetti's tone rather too tremulous for comfort, skating a little close to self-pity; but the lines are nonetheless impressive in their sad dignity. The last line is forced by the exigencies of the metre into altering the more predictable 'too late' into 'late', which has a slightly curious effect: it surely won't just be *late* for him to give her advice after she is dead, unless he is an accomplished table rapper. And it is hard to see how he could not understand this, unless he is of exceedingly low intelligence.

Another, somewhat neglected formal category is pace. Some poems creep, some jog sedately along, while others hurtle hectically forward. A piece like Browning's 'How They Brought the Good News from Ghent to Aix' moves so rapidly that it is hard to keep up with it:

> I sprang to the stirrup, and Joris, and he;
> I galloped, Dirck galloped, we galloped all three;
> 'Good speed!' cried the watch, as the gate-bolts undrew;
> 'Speed!' echoed the wall to us galloping through . . .

Percy Bysshe Shelley's 'Ode to the West Wind' swirls like wind itself:

> O wild West Wind, thou breath of Autumn's being,
> Thou, from whose unseen presence the leaves dead
> Are driven, like ghosts from an enchanter fleeing,
>
> Yellow, and black, and pale, and hectic red,
> Pestilence-stricken multitudes: O thou,
> Who chariotest to their dark wintry bed
>
> The wingèd seeds, where they lie cold and low . . .

The enjambement between the stanzas is needed to keep the wind gusting without even the briefest lull. And this single whirlwind of a sentence is sustained over more than five stanzas, as the sub-clauses sweep restively hither and thither.

Compare this, then, with the mesmerically slow pace of Tennyson's 'The Lotus Eaters':

> 'Courage!' he said, and pointed toward the land,
> 'This mounting wave will roll us shoreward soon'.
> In the afternoon they came unto a land

In which it seemed always afternoon.
All round the coast the languid air did swoon,
Breathing like one that hath a weary dream.
Full-faced above the valley stood the moon;
And, like a downward smoke, the slender stream
Along the cliff to fall and pause and fall did seem.

This tries rather too wilfully to create a mood of lethargy, all the way from the repetition of 'afternoon', with its effect of stasis and sterile circularity, to the languid alexandrine of the last line (always a risky kind of metre in English). The close-packed, sonorously recurrent rhymes (*ababbcbcc*) contribute to the sense of getting nowhere, if delectably so. No sooner do the rhymes creep forward an inch than they seem to lapse listlessly back upon themselves.

5.5   Texture

Tennyson's stanza also provides a convenient example of what we might call texture. 'Texture', which the dictionary defines as the feel or appearance of a surface or substance, is a matter of how a poem weaves its various sounds into palpable patterns. True to its indolent mood, this stanza from 'The Lotus Eaters' generally avoids sharp consonants (apart from 'pointed' and 'pause', the *p* sound of which is known as a plosive) in favour of softer, more sibilant sounds, along with a high vowel count. You can read the lines aloud without an inordinate amount of lip-work, thus re-enacting the somnolent state they portray.

Or look at the final, superb stanza of Yeats's 'Among School Children':

Labour is blossoming or dancing where
The body is not bruised to pleasure soul,
Nor beauty born out of its own despair,
Nor blear-eyed wisdom out of midnight oil.
O chestnut-tree, great-rooted blossomer,
Are you the leaf, the blossom or the bole?
O body swayed to music, O brightening glance,
How can we know the dancer from the dance?

Unlike 'The Lotus Eaters', there is a great deal of busy consonantal activity going on in this opulent tapestry of sound, not least an extraordinarily numerous set of *b* sounds ('blossoming', 'body', 'bruised', 'beauty', 'born', 'blear-eyed', 'blossomer', 'bole', 'brightening'). Yet they are not particularly obtrusive, as though the poetry is innocently unaware of them; and this is partly because they are subtly interwoven with a variety of other sounds, as in that marvellous line 'Nor blear-eyed wisdom out of midnight oil'. 'Blear' picks up the sound of 'nor', but with a pleasurable difference, while 'night' reflects the vowel sound of 'eyed'. There are also some finely accomplished semi-rhymes – 'soul' / 'oil' / 'bole', 'despair' / 'blossomer'.

Texture is also an important aspect of Thomas Hardy's poetry, as in the first verse of 'The Darkling Thrush':

> I leaned upon a coppice gate
> When Frost was spectre-grey,
> And Winter's dregs made desolate
> The weakening eye of day.
> The tangled bine-stems scored the sky
> Like strings of broken lyres,
> And all mankind that haunted nigh
> Had sought their household fires.

Even without close analysis, it is surely clear how close-packed or densely woven the sound texture is here, with every syllable in this lean verse being encouraged to work overtime. The whole stanza, highly compressed yet utterly lucid, is without an ounce of surplus fat. In the third and fourth lines, for example, the alliteration of 'Winter's' and 'weakening', and 'dregs' and 'desolate' is counterpointed by the less intrusive assonance of 'made' and 'day', along with the semi-assonance of the last syllable of 'Winter's' and the 're' sound of 'dregs'. That unmelodious 'tangled bine-stems' is chock-full of muscular syllables rammed haphazardly up against each other, a cluster of sharply diverse sounds which the reader has to work especially hard at before being rewarded with the more easily consumable consorting of 'scored' and 'sky'. The whole passage is remarkable for its tight interweaving of abstract allegory and keenly observed naturalistic detail.

5.6   Syntax, Grammar and Punctuation

A good many poetic effects are achieved through syntax. Like grammar, this has the advantage of being more 'objective' than tone or mood, and thus more easily demonstrable in its workings. Consider the opening lines of Edward Thomas's 'Old Man':

Old Man, or Lad's-love – in the name there's nothing
To one that knows not Lad's-love, or Old Man,
The hoar-green feathery herb, almost a tree,
Growing with rosemary and lavender.
Even to one that knows it well, the names
Half decorate, half perplex, the thing it is:
At least, what that is clings not to the names
In spite of time. And yet I like the names.

The herb itself I like not, but for certain
I love it, as some day the child will love it
Who plucks a feather from the door-side bush
Whenever she goes in or out of the house. . . .

One striking feature of these lines is the way they are so courageously pre-
pared to sacrifice elegance to honesty. The jagged, knotted syntax struggles
to unpack the poet's constantly swerving thoughts about the plant he is con-
templating. As it does so, its hesitations, stops and starts and doublings-back
act out something of the convolutions and self-qualifications of his response
to the herb. Syntax is pressed into the service of a tenacious commitment to
truth, as each proposition threatens to cancel out the previous claim in a dogged
struggle to pin down just what the speaker feels. A plain exactitude is all: the
herb is 'almost' a tree, but not quite; the names 'half' decorate and 'half'
perplex, but not entirely so. 'At least' then instantly qualifies that statement,
and the stumbling, unmelodious monosyllables of the line in which it occurs
– 'At least what that is clings not to the names' – are ready to risk clumsi-
ness for the sake of a rigorous truthfulness.

This statement, in turn, is then immediately qualified by 'And yet . . .'
The poet, with the perversity of his trade, likes the names but not the
herb itself, we learn to our bemusement as we step across that break in the
lines; and this is so abrupt a turnaround that it comes through as a mildly
dramatic *élan*, a kind of mischievous pulling-out of the carpet from under
the too-credulous reader. Punctuation co-operates in this ceaseless, unstable
revision of response, as the first few lines of the poem seem positively over-
loaded with commas, one of which rather redundantly backs up a dash. The
poet simply isn't certain enough of how he feels about the herb to produce
a smoothly unfractured sentence about it. Instead, one scrupulously qualifying sub-clause tumbles hard on the heels of another. It is the candour of the
passage which is part of its attraction – the way that the poet lets us see his
doubts, shifts of viewpoint and sudden modulations of feeling as they occur
to him, without feeling the need to smooth this ungainly process into an

integrated pattern. It is as though he has left the untidy stitches on his tapestry visible.

Yeats, once again, may serve as another illustration of the adroit use of syntax:

> Under my window-ledge the waters race,
> Otters below and moor-hens on the top,
> Run for a mile undimmed in Heaven's face
> Then darkening through 'dark' Raftery's 'cellar' drop,
> Run underground, rise in a rocky place
> In Coole demesne, and there to finish up
> Spread to a lake and drop into a hole.
> What's water but the generated soul?
>
> ('Coole Park and Ballylee, 1931')

The verse, as polished as Thomas's lines are irregular, almost deliberately provokes us into belletristic waffle about how beautifully the sinuous curving of the syntax mimes the flow of the stream. In a magisterial sweep, Yeats propels a single sentence around the corners and through the syntactical thickets of seven lines of poetry, pausing fractionally to register the quotation marks around 'dark' and 'cellar', without for a moment losing his poise. The last line, with its artful change of key, is a kind of final flourish to this masterly performance, with its look-no-hands bravura. It is as though the line is there to show that the poet has some breath left in him even after this virtuoso display.

We might, however, feel disconcerted by the calculated dramatic shift in the last line from the topographical to the metaphysical. One obvious riposte to that rather cavalier rhetorical question 'What's water but the generated soul?' has just been provided by the poem itself, in the shape of a detailed description of a landscape. Are we now supposed to imagine that all this was merely symbolic? The last line risks a certain glibness, a too-easy conversion of reality to allegory. It is purely assertive. We might also feel that the whole *tour de force* of the stanza is excessively deft – that it subdues this tumultuous flow rather too effortlessly to a single shapely narrative. But it is syntactical structure put to superb poetic use.

Grammar is part of the scaffolding of a poem, but it can also function as a poetic device in its own right. The first verse of T. S. Eliot's 'Whispers of Immortality' provides a convenient example:

> Webster was much possessed by death
> And saw the skull beneath the skin;
> And breastless creatures underground
> Leaned backward with a lipless grin.

Critics have argued the toss over the significance of that 'leaned'.[3] Does the meaning of the verse fall into two halves, so that we learn first that Webster was much possessed by death and saw the skull beneath the skin, and then, as a separate piece of information, that breastless creatures underground leaned backward with a lipless grin? This would make 'leaned' the past tense of 'lean'. This reading of the poem is reinforced by the presence of the semicolon at the end of line 2, which would seem to mark the one idea off from the other. But it makes for a slight strain as well, since there doesn't seem to any grammatical relation between the two ideas, even if that 'And' in the third line leads us to expect one. It would be rather like saying: 'My grandmother was a career criminal, and a bumble bee settled on my nose.'

So we could read the verse instead as a single unit of meaning: perhaps 'breastless creatures underground' is the object of 'saw', just as 'the skull beneath the skin' is. Maybe Webster saw them both. But what then do we make of 'leaned'? One suggestion is that this is not the past tense of 'lean' but the past participle, as in 'The broom was leaned against the fridge.' The breastless creatures are leaned backward, rather than engaging in the act of leaning backward. But then it is harder to make sense of the semicolon. If the creatures do not lean back by their own motion, this might very slightly diminish the horror of this macabre image, since then they appear not so nightmarishly alive. One wonders, incidentally, what is so horrific about the creatures lacking breasts, since men and children lack breasts, too, at least of the adult female kind. Is the gruesome point that they are females who have had their breasts lopped off?

5.7 Ambiguity

There is perhaps an ambiguity in this verse, then; and such ambiguity is built into the nature of poetry. This is partly because, as we have seen already, poems do not come readily equipped with material contexts to help delimit their possibilities of meaning. But it is also because, being 'semantically saturated', their meanings are often highly compressed, which may make them more difficult to unravel. An example can be found in Gerard Manley Hopkins's beautiful little lyric 'Spring and Fall', which is about a young girl weeping over the transience of human existence. The speaker tells her, by way of rather

---

[3] I am indebted for some of this discussion of the word to William Empson, *Seven Types of Ambiguity* (Harmondsworth, 1961), pp. 78–9.

backhanded consolation, that she will be less sensitive to such matters when she grows up, and then adds: 'And yet you *will* weep and know why'. William Empson, following his mentor I. A. Richards, points out that this line can have a whole number of meanings, some of which can be laid out here:

> And yet you insist on weeping, and you know why you do.
> And yet you insist on weeping, and you also insist on knowing why.
> And yet you insist on weeping, and know why! (Listen, I'm about to tell you!)
> And yet you will weep in the future, and you know why you will.
> And yet you will weep in the future, and you will know then why you do.
> And yet you will weep in the future, and know why! (Let me tell you!)

Empson discerns other possibilities, too.[4] I think the line actually means 'And yet you insist on weeping, and you also insist on knowing why.' The fact that the first 'will' is in italics makes one of the first three options more likely than any of the last three. Yet there is nothing to rule out any of these alternative readings.

It is worth noticing the difference between ambiguity and ambivalence. Ambivalence happens when we have two meanings, both of which are determinate but which differ from one another. Ambiguity happens when two or more senses of a word merge into each other to the point where the meaning itself becomes indeterminate. Alexander Pope uses the word 'port' jokingly at one point in his poetry to mean both 'harbour' and an alcoholic drink, which as a simple pun is an example of ambivalence. James Joyce's *Finnegans Wake*, by contrast, is full of words which conflate different meanings to the point of indeterminacy, as in 'the firewaterloover returted with such a vinesmelling fortytudor ages rawdownhams tanyouhide as would the latten stomach even of a tumass equinous', the meaning of which is not entirely clear.

An example of ambiguity can be found in Philip Larkin's 'Days':

> What are days for?
> Days are where we live.
> They come, they waken us
> Time and time over.
> They are to be happy in:
> Where can we live but days?

[4] See ibid., p. 148.

> Ah, solving that question
> Brings the priest and the doctor
> In their long gowns
> Running over the fields.

There is an implicit play here on the idea of time and space. Days are slices of time, but we live in them as we might inhabit a space. And running across a field is a matter of speeding up time in order to shrink space. The second verse is a masterpiece of bare suggestiveness, pivoting so much on a single spare image which is nevertheless compellingly visualisable. Without rubbing its spareness in our faces, the verse gets away with as little as it decently can, while somehow managing to make that pregnant phrase 'in their long gowns' resonant of a lot more than itself. But are the priest and the doctor running to bring comfort and counsel to this metaphysical questioner, or are they oppressive, Blakeian figures rushing to bind him into a straitjacket? The phrase 'running over the fields' has faintly sinister undertones: we do not associate respectable, long-gowned figures with such unseemly scampering. Is there an implication of panic here, as the middle-class guardians of ortho-doxy are pitched into crisis? The rural fields and the long gowns perhaps hint at a traditional, pre-modern community, for which such meaning-of-life inquiries may appear impious. So we do not know in what tone to read the last verse, whether grim or equable.

A particularly fine ambiguity occurs in the opening lines of Shakespeare's 138th sonnet:

> When my love swears that she is made of truth
> I do believe her, though I know she lies . . .

Apart from its obvious meaning, this could also mean 'When my love swears that she is truly a maid (virgin), I do believe her, though I know she lies (has sexual intercourse).'

There is also the celebrated ambiguity of Shakespeare's 94th sonnet. Here is the poem in full:

> They that have power to hurt and will do none,
> That do not do the thing they most do show,
> Who, moving others, are themselves as stone,
> Unmoved, cold, and to temptation slow,
> They rightly do inherit Heaven's graces,
> And husband nature's riches from expense;
> They are the lords and owners of their faces,

> Others but stewards of their excellence.
> The summer's flow'r is to the summer sweet
> Though to itself it only live and die;
> But if that flow'r with base infection meet,
> The basest weed outbraves his dignity:
>> For sweetest things turn sourest by their deeds;
>> Lilies that fester smell far worse than weeds.

Reading through the sonnet, we begin to wonder whether the speaker is praising the person he is addressing, or censuring him, or both. The root of the ambiguity is surely that the speaker is trying to turn what could well be seen as vices in his lover (if that is who he is talking about) into virtues. Conversely, what might sound like virtues could be vices. The Macbeth witches' 'Fair is foul and foul is fair' might thus serve as the sonnet's slogan. Having the power to hurt yet not hurting sounds admirable; but if commending this also means congratulating people who do not do the thing they most do show, it seems to involve paying tribute to hypocrisy. Men and women who are slow to temptation sound praiseworthy, but we are troubled by that 'stone' and 'cold', as well as by the feeling that there is something exploitative about stirring others' feelings while remaining imperturbable oneself.

Likewise, inheriting Heaven's graces and husbanding nature's riches from expense seem positive attainments; but if this makes you a lord and owner of your face, a kind of proprietor or entrepreneur of your self, we are suddenly not so convinced that it is entirely estimable. If we have read much Shakespeare, we might be aware that he seems generally to disapprove of this new-fangled, bourgeois idea of self-proprietorship or possessive individualism, in which it is 'as if a man were author of himself / And knew no other kin' (*Coriolanus*). Shakespeare usually regards this fantasy of self-authorship, in which one sunders all blood ties and communal affiliations, as deeply destructive. Ulysses in *Troilus and Cressida* remarks to Achilles that 'no man is the lord of anything . . . Till he communicate his parts to others', a claim which would seem to make identity without relationship a kind of cipher. It is good to know that the summer's flower is sweet to the summer, though rather more disquieting to hear that it lives and dies only to itself, which makes it sound rather unpleasantly self-absorbed.

The trouble is that we cannot simply balance positive against negative here, since we have the uneasy suspicion that the two are sides of the same coin. If this is so, then the sonnet's vision is (in an exact rather than sloppy sense of the word) dialectical. It seems as though the flower is sweet to the summer not in spite of living only for itself, but because of it; and that for it to break out of this narcissistic condition, which would appear a valuable emancipation in itself, might well involve its becoming infected. Relating to others makes you vulnerable to moral contamination, or even to some less comfortably abstract form of defilement like venereal disease; and this means that you might end up worse off than if you had stuck to your frigid self-enclosedness. Indeed, you might well end up worse off than most people would in the same circumstances, since the fact that you are so aloof and self-absorbed means that you don't have much experience of relationships, and are therefore more likely to be exploited or end up in an emotional mess than those who do. Lilies that fester smell far worse than weeds. The high-minded, if they take a tumble, are likely to make a greater splash than those without such moral pretensions.

So the speaker is arguing that a split between how you are and how you appear, which is usually regarded as a moral defect, may in fact be a virtue. Those, for example, who are sexually attractive but don't capitalise on the fact, are creditable versions of hypocrites. In any case, they are not really responsible for the desire they arouse in others, even though it may be precisely their standoffishness which provokes it. And emotional frigidity is not as reprehensible as it might seem if the consequence of it is to keep you out of temptation. Even a repellent sort of vanity or self-love may at least prevent you from injuring others. And though narcissism is sterile, other people may get something out of it (the summer's flower is sweet to the summer), so that it is not quite as worthless as it might appear.

Even so, it seems a touch hyperbolic to describe people like this as inheriting Heaven's graces, and 'husband(ing) nature's riches from expense'. Shakespeare likes the idea of good husbandry or stewardship because it involves preserving and expending in judicious measure, as opposed to being profligate with oneself, as some of his characters are, or jealously hoarding oneself, as other of his figures do. If you are spendthrift with your self then you give it away so recklessly that you end up with no self to bestow; whereas if you hoard yourself you also end up without an identity, since Shakespeare seems to agree with Ulysses that human identity is a relational affair. The icily self-possessed men and women he is portraying here sound as though they belong firmly to the second category; but the verse, perversely intent on idealising certain deficiencies, makes it appear as though they fall into the category of judicious stewards.

'Other but stewards of their excellence' now shifts the role of steward, which lurks unstated behind the verb 'husband', to the colleagues of the frigid brigade. But there is an ambiguity here: does 'their' excellence mean that of the emotionally autistic people, or that of those around them? The line could mean that whereas the frigid people are fully in command of their own resources, those around them merely benefit from these resources in a second-hand, mediated sort of way. They cannot own the self-possessed people as these individuals own themselves, and so are reduced to the rank of servants or stewards in relation to them. Perhaps they bathe in their reflected glory, and thus make use of their talents without being proprietors of them, as a steward might. Or perhaps the line means that whereas stonily unmoved people appear to own themselves, other people relate to themselves like stewards, tapping into their own powers and talents but without, so to speak, actually having the title deeds to them. This, one would gather from the rest of Shakespeare's writing, is the sort of condition of which he would approve; but here, once more, the sonnet sounds less in two minds about this way of living than we suspect that its author might actually be. There are some definite hints of disingenuousness. The piece is like a guileful speech for the defence by a counsel who knows that his client is guilty.

Why does the poet seem to be intent on making the best of a bad job? We might speculate that the sonnet is written about his lover, and meant to be read by him or her, so that it is really an indirect form of address. Perhaps, as William Empson conjectures, the lover is in some kind of danger, and the speaker is rather desperately trying to prevent him from some foolhardy involvement by praising his imperfections. This might be a more persuasive tactic than appealing to his virtues, which may be in embarrassingly scant supply. The lover should realise that his narcissism is a strength and refuse to compromise it. Or perhaps the distraught poet is trying forlornly to rationalise to himself his lover's airy indifference. In this case, it is as though he himself is being thrust into the ignoble position of a bad steward, squandering his self-possession, and thus may be implicitly contrasting his lover's coolness with the grovelling, weed-like condition to which this haughtiness has reduced him.

Maybe the lover is being tempted to go off with someone else, and the sonnet is the speaker's sophistical strategy for arguing him out of it. He may contract a moral or physical disease if he does so, thus losing the chilly self-possession which is his most alluring feature. To act would be to undo himself, ruining the very qualities which make him so easy on the eye. This is why he would resemble a festering lily. The speaker may be letting his partner know in a flagrantly self-interested sort of way (though it may also be the truth) that only by not yielding himself to his new lover will he be able to keep that lover on the hook. He may even be hoping that his partner will be so impressed by this commendation of what seems most defective about him that he will abandon his new lover and fall back into bed with his old partner. The poet is cloaking his amorous self-interest in just the kind of noble altruism which might turn his lover on. Or perhaps there is no such rhetorical situation at stake, and the sonnet is simply remarking on the irony by which even our vices can turn out to be perversely virtuous.

If the lover has been in some way trifling with the poet's affections, something similar may be said of the poem's relation to the reader. Its technique is to keep the reader guessing, catch her on the hop, refuse to sediment into a single, unequivocal attitude. And this seems a kind of poetic equivalent to erotic teasing, no sooner offering us a crumb of comfort than swapping it for a poisoned barb. We are uncertain where the poet actually stands, but this may not be because the poem is exactly ironic. It may be investigating what we might call an 'objective' irony, but it does not follow that it does not mean what it says. Maybe Shakespeare is perfectly sincere in believing that to be lord and owner of oneself may be to diminish the degree of human damage one might wreak. It is just that he also probably believes – outside the confines of the poem, so to speak – that there is also much that is undesirable about such self-lordship. But there is no reason why he has to say that here, even if the phrase 'are themselves as stone' hints at it almost too heavily. Nobody, not even Shakespeare, has to say everything at once.

5.8   Punctuation

One of the most neglected formal techniques is punctuation. It is puzzling, for example, why there should be an exclamation mark after the lines from Eliot's 'Whispers of Immortality' which read: 'Daffodil bulbs instead of balls / Stared from the sockets of the eyes!' Exclamation marks are clumsy markers of emotion for such a suavely adept poet as Eliot. They are naive, usually superfluous, and almost always overemphatic. So one suspects that this one is somehow ironic, though it is hard to see how. It is, so to speak, in quotation marks. There is a tender lyric by e. e. cummings which ends with this verse:

> (i do not know what it is about you that closes
> and opens;only something in me understands
> the voice of your eyes is deeper than all roses)
> nobody,not even the rain, has such small hands
> ('somewhere I have never travelled, gladly beyond')

cummings often leaves out punctuation marks altogether, or, as here, squeezes them between words as though he wants them to be as unobtrusive as possible. (This actually makes them more obtrusive.) One can see why he doesn't want a full stop after 'roses' or 'hands': it would be too forceful, definitive a gesture for such delicate, gossamer-like verse, which may also be one reason why the poet avoids capital letters. (A less reputable reason may be the assumption that 'onion' is democratic whereas 'Onion' is elitist.) Full stops would chop up into discrete units of meaning what is intended as a series of fragile, tentative statements. They would end-stop his feelings. But in that case he might have been better off without those commas in the last line, leaving it to the reader to introduce the pauses. The title of the poem is also its first line, and one sees why it needs that comma: without it, it might sound as though he means 'somewhere I have never travelled gladly', which given the meaning of the poem's first lines would be something of a slap in the face for his lover. But it is a pity, all the same, that the comma should have to intrude.

cummings also uses colons, semicolons and commas in the body of the poem that could have been omitted. (Colons, incidentally, have today almost passed out of existence, along with string vests and sideburns.) If you want an effect of perpetual open-endedness you can leave the line-endings to do the work of pausing, rather than full-stop them. The verse puts its first three lines in parenthesis, as though they are a kind of musing aside; and this also has the added bonus of throwing that poignant final line into relief, since it is the only unbracketed one in the stanza. The synaesthesia of 'the voice of your eyes is deeper than all roses' is not quite as accomplished: eyes deeper than all roses is an imaginative conceit, or even a voice deeper than all roses, though that is rather too literal to be quite as effective; but 'the voice of your eyes' is surely just incongruous.

5.9 Rhyme

Rhyme is one of the most familiar of all technical devices, and we have seen a good deal of it so far. Perhaps it reflects the fact that we take a childlike delight in doublings, mirror images and affinities, which have something magical (but also something disquieting and uncanny) about them. There is pleasure to be reaped from repetition: small children tend to go on repeating well beyond the point that most adults find tolerable. In its predictability, repetition may yield us a sense of security. For Freudians, it reflects the natural indolence of the psyche – the fact that left to ourselves, without the goad of economic necessity, we would simply lounge around the place all day in various scandalous states of *jouissance*. We do not like to expend too much libidinal energy, and repetition is one way in we can 'bind' such energy and thus avoid an excess of expenditure. It is true that too much repetition is tedious, but rhyme can overcome this danger because it is a unity of identity and difference. We hear 'dragon' and 'wagon' as akin, but also as dissimilar.

Perhaps because modern life is felt to be somehow dissonant, a good many poets begin to abandon the use of rhyme as we enter the modern age. Or, like the First World War poet Wilfred Owen, they compromise by using para-rhyme, words which almost chime in unison but don't quite:

> Happy are men who yet before they are killed
> Can let their veins run cold.
> Whom no compassion fleers
> Or makes their feet
> Sore on the alleys cobbled with their brothers.
> The front line withers.
> But they are troops who fade, not flowers,
> For poet's tearful fooling:
> Men, gaps for filling:
> Losses, who might have fought
> Longer: but no one bothers.
> ('Insensibility')

There is a mourning, haunting, almost eerie quality to these superbly invent-ive para-rhymes: 'killed'/'cold', 'fleers'/'flowers', 'feet'/'fought', 'fooling'/'filling', 'brothers'/'withers'/'bothers'. Everything is discomfortingly awry, off-key, out of kilter, as one might expect from a writer living through unimaginable human carnage. One imagines that full-blooded rhyme would seem a kind of false harmony to a poet like this, who has been reduced by the horrors of war to actually commending insensitivity and the conscious blunting of compassion. One can imagine the scandalised reaction of many a Victorian to this humane counsel.

'Cobbled' is brutal in its dehumanising force, its impact intensified by the fact that it is a sudden image in lines which have been so far fairly free of them. But the casual savagery of the term has to be held in tension with 'brothers'. It is not that the soldiers are not as much brothers as ever, just that they cannot afford the kind of sentimentality which would say so. Feeling can kill: any too-powerful emotion is likely to make the soldiers more vulnerable to their situation, and thus to intensify its dreadfulness. It is callousness here which is compassionate. This applies to 'Insensibility' as well as to the troops: one can sense its deep-seated anger, but also the icy control which throttles it back so that the poem can take place.

'Insensibility' even lip-curlingly denies its own status as poetry, which in these conditions can be no more than tearful fooling. As a piece of stony-hearted anti-poetry, it is in conflict with itself (though it is also meticulously crafted). It goes out of its way to take a smack at metaphor, even though 'cobbled with their brothers' is precisely that. Its language, for such a sensuous poet as Owen, is ascetic and austere. The line 'The front line withers' stands starkly isolated and end-stopped, four laconic words marooned at the verse's centre. It is as though any attempt to elaborate this bald fact would be a lie. If the rhymes are off-key, so is the metre, which shifts between lines of varying numbers of feet. The final phrase of the verse – 'but no one bothers' – contrasts the unavoidable anaesthesia of those plunged in the thick of warfare with the rather more culpable insensitivity of those kicking their heels comfortably at home, not least perhaps the politicians who sent the soldiers there. Insensibility applies to both groups, but for quite different reasons.

While we are on the subject of war poetry, it is worth contrasting Owen's poem with John McCrae's 'In Flanders Fields':

> In Flanders fields the poppies blow
> Between the crosses, row on row,
>   That mark our place; and in the sky
>   The larks, still bravely singing, fly
> Scarce heard amid the guns below.
>
> We are the Dead. Short days ago
> We lived, felt dawn, saw sunset glow,
>   Loved and were loved, and now we lie,
>   In Flanders fields.
>
> Take up our quarrel with the foe:
> To you from failing hands we throw
>   The torch; be yours to hold it high.
>   If ye break faith with us who die
> We shall not sleep, though poppies grow
>   In Flanders fields.

Perhaps this is the kind of war poem Owen had in his sights, though it is hardly tearful fooling. There is a jauntiness about the metre (an iambic tetrameter) which is at odds with the tragedy of the war, though perhaps not so much at odds with the martial clarion-call of the final verse. Far from exploiting the dissonance of para-rhyme, the piece (if one leaves aside the refrain) rings changes on only two rhyming sounds, thus generating a peculiarly close-knit rhyme scheme. This creates a faintly chant-like effect – one which again seems askew to the sombre feeling, but which fits well enough with the poem's rousing last lines.

What the lines say is that the dead will only feel vindicated if those left alive create even more corpses, a bloodthirsty demand for such a noble-spirited elegy. It is hard to square the piece's high-minded mournfulness with its call to arms, which is too close to vengeance for comfort. It is not the kind of sentiment one can imagine Wilfred Owen easily endorsing; indeed, it sounds like that of a non-combatant safely ensconced behind the lines. But McCrae was in fact a Canadian soldier who survived some of the bloodiest episodes of the war. It is not clear why the dead soldiers might not sleep even though poppies grow above them, unless the allusion is to the poppies' opiate effect. But it seems incongruous and undignified to suggest that the dead warriors are sleeping because they are doped.

Finally, it is worth glancing at the Second-World War author John Pudney's celebrated piece 'For Johnny', with its tight *aa/bb* rhyme scheme:

> Do not despair
> For Johnny-head-in-air;
> He sleeps as sound
> As Johnny underground.
>
> Fetch out no shroud
> For Johnny-in-the-cloud;
> And keep your tears
> For him in after years.
>
> Better by far
> For Johnny-the-bright-star,
> To keep your head,
> And see his children fed.

These terse lines, to be delivered with an officer-like crispness of accent, struggle so hard to avoid sentimentality that they lapse right into it, in a bravely-choking-back-emotion sort of way. And the rhyme scheme is among other things a way of mastering the emotion. Throttling back feeling can be a perverse way of stimulating it, as with the Dickensian type of rough-diamond sentimentalist who reaps a secret *frisson* from pretending to be gruff. It is the very tight-lipped disowning of feeling here which comes through as a lump in the throat. Yet the poem is impressive in a kitschy kind of way. It is a fair specimen of a disreputable species, hovering between genuine emotional power and barely-suppressed sentimentality. It is also an example of pragmatically effective verse: no doubt it consoled a good many families who had lost sons and husbands in the war. It is saddening, even so, to learn that the author of this gem, which Laurence Oliver read on wartime radio and Michael Redgrave quoted in a patriotic film, was also the author of *The Smallest Room*, a history of the lavatory.

5.10   Rhythm and Metre

Rhythm in poetry is not the same as metre. Metre is a regular pattern of stressed and unstressed syllables, whereas rhythm is less formalised. It means the irregular sway and flow of the verse, its ripplings and undulations as it follows the flexing of the speaking voice. Much of the effect of English-language poetry comes from playing the one off against the other. Shylock's line in Shakespeare's *The Merchant of Venice* –

How like a fawning publican he looks!

– is an iambic pentameter, with the following pattern of stresses (the syllables in bold type being the stressed ones):

How **like** a **fawn**ing **publ**ican he **looks**!

An actor who delivered the line like this, however, would no doubt receive a less than rapturous response from the audience. Instead, he might articulate it like this:

How like a fawning **publ**ican he **looks**!

which clings to the curve of the speaking voice. But the metre leaves open various possibilities. Its beat can be heard as a dim throbbing behind the actual delivery, forming a stable background against which the freestyle acrobatics of the voice can stand out. It is as though metre supplies the score on which rhythm improvises.

Rhythm is one of the most 'primordial' of poetic features. It can be a simple matter of tripping and lilting, or it can well up from a much deeper psychic level, as a pattern of motion and impulse which is inherited from our earliest years, which has tenacious somatic and psychological roots, and which is imprinted in the folds and textures of the self. A baby of six months cannot talk, but scientists have established that it can detect subtle variations in the complex rhythmic patterns of Balkan folk-dance tunes. And it can do so even if it is born in Boston.

A poem by Walter Raleigh shows just how beautifully sinuous and flexible poetic rhythm can be:

> As you came from the holy land
> of Walsinghame
> Mett you not with my true love
> by the way as you came
> How shall I know your trew love
> That has met many one
> As I went to the holy lande
> That have come, that have gone . . .
>
>   ('As You Came from the Holy Land')

That delicately lilting second line, consisting as it does of just two words, comes as a wonderfully subtle rhythmical modulation after the more conventional metre of the first line. As we shift from line to line, we move in a kind of fine surprise from one set of cunningly varied rhythmic impulses to another. If the sense is continuous, the rhythmic units which go to make it up are delightfully diverse and unpredictable.

Something similar can be said of Stevie Smith's legendary 'Not Waving But Drowning':

> Nobody heard him, the dead man,
> But still he lay moaning:
> I was much further out than you thought
> And not waving but drowning.
>
> Poor chap, he always loved larking
> And now he's dead
> It must have been too cold for him his heart gave way,
> They said.
>
> Oh, no no no, it was too cold always
> (Still the dead one lay moaning)
> I was much too far out all my life
> And not waving but drowning.

The first stanza alternates lines of three stresses with lines of two, a pattern which the second two stanzas sustain in a more irregular way. The effect of this is a kind of rise and fall, or a shift from a major to a minor key, as the more expansive line is followed up by the more downbeat, diminished one. A sense of bathos lurks behind this device, one which informs the poem as a whole: from the tragedy of drowning to the triviality of waving is a mere nuance of perception. The two keywords, 'waving' and 'drowning', are dissonant but vaguely reminiscent of each other, as though from a distance one could mistake the one for the other, just as from the beach one can confuse the actual gestures.

The first two lines of the second stanza conform to the metrical pattern of the first, as bathos breaks out again with that comically matter-of-fact 'And now he's dead'; but with 'It must have been too cold for him his heart gave way, / They said' the rhythm goes grotesquely awry. One would expect this clumsily lurching line to be broken up into two neatly balanced ones ('It must have been too cold for him, / His heart gave way, they said'), but Smith wants to get a sense of the dead man's companions' flurried, disorganised chatter. Like a breathless snatch of gossip, the line lacks punctuation. It has the clumping lack of symmetry of everyday speech. Smith also wants to create a ridiculous effect, deflating the high drama of the drowning by ineptly crowding this cack-handed line with too many words, as though the stanza has suddenly bucked out of her control. Then, after this ridiculously gauche line, one which captures the *faux-naïf* quality of the poem as a whole, we have bathos once more, with the lame trailing-off of 'They said' being incongruously allotted a whole line to itself. The swimmer even muffs the big moment of his death, unable to rise to the grandeur of the tragic; and the verse follows suit by disastrously losing its sense of rhythm.

The final stanza is spoken by the drowned man himself (there are three interweaving voices in this brief poem), and devalues his death even further by suggesting that it is really not much different from his life. His explanation, however, has come too late: nobody hears him in death, just as nobody heard him in life. Perhaps this is not entirely the fault of the friends: perhaps he really did lark about, as a way of proudly concealing the fact that he was in trouble, and so is partly responsible for the farcical misinterpretation which was his existence. The poem beautifully blends comedy and poignancy.

Let us look finally at a poem by a distinguished, unduly neglected poet of eighteenth-century Ireland, William Dunkin. Dunkin's finest piece is entitled 'The Parson's Revels', and is couched in a very rare stanza form:[5]

> His voice was brazen, deep, and such,
> As well-accorded with High-dutch,
> Or Attic Irish, and his touch
>   Was pliant;

[5] It is, however, to be found in a bawdy poem called 'The Ramble' by the English Restoration poet Alexander Radcliffe, which rhymes 'clitoris' with 'Tell stories'.

> Dubourgh to him was but a fool;
> He played melodious without rule,
> And sung the feats of Fin McCool,
>   The giant . . .

The rhyme scheme in the poem is a kind of comic ritual in itself. Dunkin uses some deliberately inept rhymes ('scurvy'/'topsy-turvy', 'from it'/ 'vomit', 'dead aunt'/'pedant'), but the real comic effect is reaped from the way the first three lines of each verse (which are iambic tetrameters) set up a rhythm which is suddenly disrupted by the final, lamely tacked-on phrase. These final phrases come after a slight pause, during which the reader just has time to wonder what monstrously over-ingenious rhyme is about to be perpetrated. The final phrase, with its brief trisyllabic lilt, is inevitably bathetic:

> Each blithesome damsel shews her shape,
> Enough to burst her stays and tape,
> And bangs the boards: the fiddlers scrape
>   Their cat-guts:
>
> Brave C–, foe to popish dogs,
> In boots, as cumbersome as clogs,
> Displays his parts, and B —jogs
>   His fat guts.

The final phrases, almost afterthoughts, are too laconic to bear the emphasis which the verse throws on them, and this itself is a comic effect. The phrases are necessary to round off the sense of each stanza, yet rhythmically speaking they seem like feebly superfluous gestures. Each stanza thus seems to end on an embarrassing anti-climax, as the speaking voice trails away. It is as though the sense needs these phrases but the metre does not, since it and its trim, triple rhyme are already complete in themselves. This tension between feeling that the phrases are internal to the verses, yet also pointlessly external to them, is a kind of wit.

5.11   Imagery

Finally, a word about imagery. Just as rhyme, metre and texture involve an interplay of difference and identity, so do most images. Similes and metaphors insist on affinities between elements which we also acknowledge to be different; and the more we attend to the kinship between the terms, the larger the differences may loom. Metonymy links elements in a contiguous way (bird/sky, for example), thus also creating an equivalence between things which we recognise to be disparate. Synecdoche substitutes a part for a whole (wing for bird, for example, or crown for monarch), and parts and wholes are both different and allied.

The term 'image' is in some ways misleading, since it suggests the visual, and not all imagery is of this kind. Auden, for example, is famous for images which yoke together the concrete and the abstract: 'Anxiety receives them like a Grand Hotel'; 'And lie apart like epochs from each other'. Part of the point of similes like this, which belong to an era in which the whole idea of representation is in crisis, is that they baffle any attempt to visualise them. But this is true in a sense of all such equating of one thing with another. We speak of similes and metaphors as images; but both of them are forms of comparison, and it is hard to see how a comparison can be a picture.[6] We can describe jealousy as a green-eyed monster, but this tends to mean that we picture a green-eyed monster rather than jealousy. You can take a photograph of a goat, but not of lechery. You can hold the two parts of the comparison together in language, just as in language you can have a purple-coloured pain, a grin without a cat, a square circle, a person who is both dead and alive, or a cathedral which is built entirely out of stone but also entirely out of jelly. But it is not easy to portray any of these phenomena visually. What image does 'My love is like a red, red rose' bring to mind? A rose with well-plucked eyebrows and dainty legs? It is language's lack of visualisability which confers such enviable freedom upon it. Seeing language as no more than an image or representation of reality is a way of restricting its liberty. In literary history, the words for such policing of the signifier are realism and naturalism – movements which, despite their exclusiveness, have been immensely fertile and productive.

It is true that there are kinds of imagery which do not involve visualisation. We speak, for example, of aural or tactile imagery. Yet the word remains more deceptive than illuminating. For some eighteenth-century critics, imagery referred to the power of poetry to make us 'see' objects, to feel as if we were in their actual presence; but this implied, oddly, that the function of poetic language was to efface itself before what it represented. Language makes things vividly present to us, but to do so adequately it must cease to interpose its own ungainly bulk between us and them. So poetic language

---

[6]   A point made by P. N. Furbank in his *Reflections on the Word 'Image'* (London, 1970), p. 1.

attains its pitch of perfection when it ceases to be language at all. At its peak, it transcends itself.

Images, on this theory, are representations so lucid that they cease to be representations at all, and instead merge with the real thing. Which means, logically speaking, that we are no longer dealing with poetry at all, which is nothing if not a verbal phenomenon. F. R. Leavis writes of the kind of verse which 'has such life and body that we hardly seem to be reading arrangements of words . . . The total effect is as if words as words withdrew themselves from the focus of our attention and we were directly aware of a tissue of feelings and perceptions.'[7] It is ironic that on this view, poetry can create the impression of real things more powerfully than the visual arts. When we gaze at a painting of a landscape, we know that what we are seeing is not the landscape itself, precisely because the painting is itself a visual object, one which distinguishes itself from what it depicts in the very act of being faithful to it. But when the medium of representation is not itself visual, as with poetry, this is not so obvious.

The idea of the 'image', which first emerges in its modern sense in the late seventeenth century, arises from the suspicion of rhetoric felt by an Age of Reason.[8] Words are not to act as slippery figures of speech, but to behave as 'images' or clear representations of things. It is ironic, then, that in some later criticism 'imagery' and 'figures of speech' come to be more or less synonymous. Modern movements like Imagism inherited this belief in clear representations, as poets like H. D. and Ezra Pound, alarmed by a commercial and bureaucratic language which seemed out of touch with concrete reality, sought to yoke words and things more tightly together. The idea of the concrete springs to the fore when reality itself seems to have become abstract. 'No ideas but in things' became William Carlos Williams's programmatic slogan. Language on this view is at its most trustworthy when it is thing-like, and thus not language at all. At its most authentic, it flips over into something else.

Imagery, then, did not originally mean such devices as metaphor and simile. In fact, it meant almost the opposite of them. The word harboured a marked hostility to figurative language, rather than denoting certain familiar uses of it. It was only with the Romantic movement, when it was accepted that even the clearest perception of the world involves the creative imagination,

---

[7] F. R. Leavis, 'Imagery and Movement: Notes in the Analysis of Poetry', *Scrutiny*, September 1945, p. 124.

[8] See R. Frazer, 'The Origin of the Word "Image"', in *English Literary History*, vol. xxvii, pp. 149–61.

that the two notions began to coalesce. What had started out as a matter of clear representations now touched on the very essence of the poetic imagination, which combines, distinguishes, unifies and transforms. Moreover, if our knowledge of reality involved the imagination, then imagery was cognitive, not merely decorative. It could no longer be dismissed as so much superfluous embellishment. Instead, it lay at the very heart of the poetic. Rhetoric and reality were no longer at daggers drawn. Metaphor was now more or less equivalent to the poetic as such. It was a supremely privileged activity of the human spirit, not just a rhetorical device.

By the middle of the nineteenth century, 'imagery' had come to mean pretty much what it means for us today. Yet what exactly *does* it mean? Some dictionaries inform us that the term means 'figurative language', in the sense of language which is non-literal. But similes are surely literal enough. There is nothing figurative in claiming that your boyfriend looks like a toad, as opposed to claiming that he *is* a toad. It is true that the word 'literal' is much abused these days, as in 'I literally fell through the floor in amazement', where the word 'literal' is itself figurative. But similes are quite literally literal. Nor is everything we call a figure of speech a non-literal use of language. This is true enough of hyperbole (exaggeration), litotes (understatement), irony, personification and so on; but what of a figure like chiasmus, in which a pattern of words is repeated in reverse order? The *Oxford English Dictionary* tells us that chiasmus is a figure, yet defines 'figure of speech' as a non-literal use of words. Are imagery and figures of speech the same thing, or is the former confined to simile and metaphor?

The theory of imagery, then, is in something of a mess. One critic informs us that 'Imagery is a form of metaphor or figurative speech, a kind of picture language.'[9] Yet on some theories, metaphor, figurative speech and picture language are either distinct or mutually incompatible. Another commentator, seeking perhaps to square the circle, defines imagery as any concrete as opposed to abstract representation in poetry, whether literal or figurative.[10] One reason why the idea of the image looms so large in the post-Romantic era is because of literature's evolving love affair with the concrete. As we have seen already, the cult of the concrete particular dates largely from this period; and images are thought to be peculiarly solid, vivid and specific. Yet this is a mistaken assumption. There are lots of similes and metaphors, not least in, say, Elizabethan poetry, which are not at all sensuously particular.

[9]   Paul Haeffner, quoted in Furbank, *Reflections*, p. 56.
[10]   See Chris Baldick, *The Concise Oxford Dictionary of Literary Terms* (Oxford and New York, 1990), p. 106. Baldick's book is an excellent guide to its subject.

You can have hazy general images as well as grippingly specific ones. In any case, as we saw in discussing Seamus Heaney, the idea that some uses of language are more concrete than others needs to be handled with care. It is true that an elaborately detailed verbal portrait of a green-eyed monster is less abstract than the concept of jealousy; but the *words* 'green-eyed monster' are not less abstract than the word 'jealousy'. No word – as opposed to an idea – is more concrete or abstract than any other.

In any case, it is a mistake to equate concreteness with things. An individual object is the unique phenomenon it is because it is caught up in a mesh of relations with other objects. It is this web of relations and interactions, if you like, which is 'concrete', while the object considered in isolation is purely abstract. In his *Grundrisse*, Karl Marx sees the abstract not as a lofty, esoteric notion, but as a kind of rough sketch of a thing. The notion of money, for example, is abstract because it is no more than a bare, preliminary outline of the actual reality. It is only when we reinsert the idea of money into its complex social context, examining its relations to commodities, exchange, production and the like, that we can construct a 'concrete' concept of it, one which is adequate to its manifold substance. The Anglo-Saxon empiricist tradition, by contrast, makes the mistake of supposing that the concrete is simple and the abstract is complex. In a similar way, a poem for Yury Lotman is concrete precisely because it is the product of many interacting systems. Like Imagist poetry, you can suppress a number of these systems (grammar, syntax, metre and so on) to leave the imagery standing proudly alone; but this is actually an abstraction of the imagery from its context, not the concretion it appears to be. In modern poetics, the word 'concrete' has done far more harm than good.

But enough of theory for the moment. It is time now to turn back to the poems themselves, in a final analysis of some well-known English verses.

Chapter 6

Four Nature Poems

6.1 William Collins, 'Ode to Evening'

In this final chapter, I want to examine some English Nature poems as a further exercise in close critical analysis. There is no particular rhyme or reason in the selection of these pieces, no obvious connections between them, and no special significance in the fact that they are all about Nature. They simply provide convenient texts to scrutinise.

The first is an extract from the eighteenth-century poet William Collins's 'Ode to Evening':

> . . . Then lead, calm votaress, where some sheety lake
> Cheers the lone heath, or some time-hallowed pile
>   Or uplands fallows gray
>   Reflect its last cool gleam.
> But when chill blustering winds, or driving rain
> Forbid my willing feet, be mine the hut
>   That from the mountain's side
>   Views wilds, and swelling floods,
> And hamlets brown, and dim-discovered spires,
> And hears their simple bell, and marks o'er all
>   Thy dewy fingers draw
>   The gradual dusky veil.

It would be hard to find a style of poetry more alien to the modern sensibility. A modern reader who can enjoy this kind of stuff has developed a genuinely catholic taste. Two aspects of this magnificent poem are immediately unattractive to the typical modern reader: its elaborately formal diction, and its solemnly elevated tone. Diction means the kind of vocabulary conventionally considered suitable for poetry; and the point about modern poetry is that there isn't one. Most modern poetry uses what we might roughly call everyday speech. It is the effects it conjures from this speech which are 'poetic', not the fact that it uses a special idiom set apart from ordinary language. Neoclassical poetry, by contrast, as the critic Donald Davie observes in his study *Purity of Diction in English Verse*, achieves some of its peculiar effects by seeming to fend off certain terms which can be felt hovering on its margins but which it would be indecorous to allow in.

Shakespeare is not constrained by diction either, plundering any sort of vocabulary that comes to hand. This is no doubt one reason why many readers today find it easier to thrill to his language than to the language of, say, John Milton. There is a feeling abroad in some quarters that the native genius of the English language is to be informal and colloquial, and that any more formalised speech is more suitable to high-toned nations like the French. This belief is sometimes accompanied by an interest in Morris dancing and flagons of warm cider.

But there are other cultural situations in which if you did not employ a quasi-technical language for poetry, what you produced would not really be counted as a poem. A great many terms would be regarded as inappropriate for poetry, perhaps because they are too 'low'. This censorship extended into the twentieth century: plenty of Georgian poets would not have contemplated using words like 'steam engine' or 'telegraph' in their work. There are, to be sure, much plainer eighteenth-century poems than 'Ode to Evening'; Collins is especially enamoured of ornate poetic figures. But these figures are by and large the kind of thing that an eighteenth-century reader would have expected from his or her volumes of verse.

The other unappealing aspect of the lines to some modern readers is their tone, which seems equally removed from everyday life. Odes like this are expected to sound reasonably exalted. We may note that this noble or dignified tone is relatively uniform: it does not modulate much in accordance with whatever it is the poem is observing, nor is it intended to. Thus, when the poet makes tracks for the humble hut to shelter from the rain, we might expect some major shift of tone, but we don't get it. Instead, we get the kind of tension between form and content that we have investigated previously. If the hut is humble, the poem's language is not. It records the 'simple' bell of the hamlets or villages in fairly lofty terms. Just as the language of the poem seems to view things from an Olympian vantage point, without detailed close-ups, so the poet makes use of his refuge in the hut for a panoramic surveillance of the landscape around him, sweeping from the sublime (mountains and swelling floods) to the modest domesticity of the hamlets (or small villages). The high and the low are also combined in the image of the church spires, which are mysteriously 'dim-discovered' yet furnished with 'simple' bells. The grandeur of this spectacle is at odds with the work-aday place from which it is observed. And this, for an eighteenth-century readership as well as for many of us today, is perfectly appropriate and acceptable.

The poet is not really part of the landscape he contemplates, and this, again, is part of its poetic decorum. It is true that he dips into the scene briefly by indulging in the fiction of being driven to seek shelter from the rain, as though to account for how he gets from one part of the terrain to another; but the device of the hut is then abandoned. For the poem is not about the poet and his wanderings, which might seem distastefully subjectivist to a neoclass-ical author like Collins. It is about Evening itself. What holds its various experiences together is not the fact that they all occur to one William Collins, which would indeed be a Romantic sort of gambit, but the fact that they are all part of a conveniently wide-ranging abstraction known as Evening. And Evening, once it has arrived, covers just about everything.

This, then, allows Collins to meander around in an apparently desultory fashion, inspecting this or that at his leisure, while ensuring, as a good neo-classical author should, that all of this adds up to a harmonious totality. He allows himself a Romantic latitude within a classical whole. These particular lines of the poem are in fact the only part of it in which the author himself puts in a personal appearance. It would be poetic bad manners to centre every-thing on himself. He does not even view the landscape himself; instead, this activity is delegated to the hut, which seems to do his viewing for him. From 'The gradual dusky veil' to the end of the poem, he effaces himself from view and disappears entirely into the poem's language, which turns in impersonal fashion to a personification of the various seasons of the year.

The ode, then, is not at all to do with the poet's unique experience of the world, as a poem by Keats might be. Nor is it meant to be. We hear very little about how the poet feels about what he observes. We are not dealing with 'consciousness' here, as we might be with Wordsworth or Thomas Hardy. Wordsworth is on the whole less concerned to give us a detailed image of Nature than a detailed map of his mind. The living, breathing, active subject of Collins's poem is not the poet but Evening, on to whom subjectivity, so to speak, is displaced. But if the poem is not particularly concerned with the human subject, neither in a sense is it to do with the natural object.

Everything its author sees is mediated by elaborate literary codes, as is clear from some earlier lines of the work:

> . . . O nymph reserved, while now the bright-haired sun
> Sits in yon western tent, whose cloudy skirts,
>   With brede ethereal wove,
>   O'erhang his wavy bed . . .

There is no direct perception here at all, and no call for it. Collins is not actually looking at anything. He does not need to peer out of his study window to call the sun bright-haired, to portray clouds as skirts, or to speak of the sea as a wavy bed. This is not the kind of verse which puts any great store by meticulous observation. We post-Romantics tend to regard this as a deficiency, but for Collins it would not have seemed so, nor need it seem so to us. He might well have considered it eccentric and indecorous to think up strikingly specific phrases which sought to capture the exact tints and surgings of the ocean.

For the greatest English eighteenth-century critic, Samuel Johnson, this would be an idle distraction from the poet's proper business of conveying general truths. It is a measure of the gulf between pre-Romantics like Johnson and post-Romantics like ourselves that Johnson found generalities deeply interesting and particularities rather pointless. Scientists might want to investigate the sun in greater detail than 'bright-haired', but there is no call for poets and moralists to do so. And this applies to the study of humanity as well: what is important are the few great things that human beings share in common, not their arbitrary deviations from this uniform nature. The specialist scrutiny of individual cases obscures the few fundamental facts about them that we need to know in order to assess their place in the great scheme of things. So terms like 'bright-haired', which seem to us a kind of poetic jargon, are also ways of avoiding jargon, in the sense of specialist language. 'Bright-haired' and 'wavy bed' tell us as much as we need to know. Conventional terms are more informative than freakishly new-fangled ones. But even these terms must not be *stalely* conventional; they must involve some degree of inventiveness on the poet's part. Later in the poem a forest becomes a 'sylvan shed', which is inventive enough.

The poem, then, is really about neither human subject nor natural object, but the medium in which they commingle, which is language itself. It is an intricate, highly artificial rhetorical exercise, even though its subject matter is supposedly Nature. The work is not meant to be 'true to Nature'; instead, Nature is made to be true to it by being recast in terms of symbol, allegory, mythology, stock literary epithets and the like. Nature itself becomes a text or aesthetic object. There is nothing very natural about it. When the poet implies that he is attracted to the simple life by heading for the hut, this is as much a poetic convention as referring to Evening's dewy fingers drawing a dusky veil. It is not that the ode is insincere: terms like 'sincere' and 'insincere' are no more applicable to it than they are to a duck's quacking, or to the carpentering of a rosewood dining table.

It has become fashionable to talk of poems as being about themselves, but in much of Collins's ode this is literally true. Almost the entire first half of the work consists of the poet appealing to Evening to teach him how to sing her praises – which means that almost half the poem is about the act of writing the poem itself. In the process of this appeal, the poem waxes lyrical about Evening, so that it does what it asks to do in the act of asking to do it. All this occurs in a single sentence of considerable syntactical complexity which stretches for twenty lines:

> If ought of oaten stop, or pastoral song,
> May hope, chaste Eve, to soothe thy modest ear,
> > Like thy own solemn springs,
> > Thy springs and dying gales,
> O nymph reserved, while now the bright-haired sun
> Sits in yon western tent, whose cloudy skirts,
> > With brede ethereal wove,
> > O'erhangs his wavy bed:
> Now air is hushed, save where the weak-eyed bat,
> With short shrill shriek flits by on leathern wing,
> > Or where the beetle winds
> > His small but sullen horn,
> As oft he rises 'midst the twilight path,
> Against the pilgrim borne in heedless hum:
> > Now teach me, maid composed,
> > To breathe some softened strain,
> Whose numbers, stealing through thy darkening vale,
> May not unseemly with its stillness suit,
> > As, musing slow, I hail
> > Thy genial loved return!

What this says in bare grammatical outline is: If you would like a song, Evening, teach me one yourself. But in saying this, the poem digresses and elaborates so much, taking a circuitous route through one sub-clause after another, that it becomes the song which it is asking to sing. The form of the poem – the performative act by which it is requesting inspiration – becomes its content. This, to be sure, involves some grammatical sleight of hand: there is a slightly awkward transition, for example, from 'O'erhangs his wavy bed' to 'Now air is hushed'. Everything up to 'wavy bed' can be read without grammatical strain as part of the poet's address to Evening, but 'Now air is hushed' shifts to a descriptive passage which really stands on its own and can't easily be folded into the act of addressing Evening. It is not clear by what logic the poem slides from the performative to the descriptive. The act of addressing Evening is taken up again in 'Now teach me, maid composed', as the poem regains its rhetorical stride after this deviation into descriptiveness.

Even so, the verbal quality of that description can be related to the self-referential act which is the poem itself. Lines like 'With short shrill shriek flits by on leathern wing' and 'His small but sullen horn' betray a high degree of linguistic self-consciousness, as though the poet has his eye on the phrase rather than the object. 'Small but sullen' is a little too fastidiously qualifying, while 'short shrill shriek' overdoes the alliteration. The ostentatious artifice of these phrases signals a self-conscious distance between the poem's language and its objects, or between art and Nature. We are reminded insistently of that art, too, in the metre's constant alternation of pentameters and trimeters, lines of five stresses and lines of three. Just as the poem curves back on itself structurally, by being about the song which is itself, so some of its more local verbal effects are peculiarly self-regarding. We are perpetually aware of the gap between the 'mind' of the poem, as expressed in its form and language, and the natural world of which it speaks. In other hands – Thomas Hardy's, for example – this gap can become the stuff of tragedy; but 'Ode to Evening' is not a tragic poem, even if its blitheness of spirit feels at times a little laboured, weighed down as it is with all that top-heavy imagery.

When the poet talks about visiting a lake on the heath, or taking refuge in a hut, he is not describing actual events, and we are not meant to imagine that he is. He is talking in a general kind of way. These are the sort of things one might typically do, not necessarily things that one actually has done or will do. Only in one or two places does Collins seem to be speaking about realities actually present to his eyes, as when he writes of the sun 'now' sitting in the sky, and then, a few lines later:

> Now air is hushed, save where the weak-eyed bat,
> With short shrill shriek flits by on leathern wing,
>   Or where the beetle winds
>   His small but sullen horn,
> As oft he rises 'midst the twilight path . . .

No sooner do we seem to occupy an actual time and place than we take leave of it again. The beetle winds his horn in the present, as 'oft' he rises on the path. What seems actual turns out to be typical or general. Collins is interested in the kind of thing beetles tend to do, not in any individual beetle. And in this he is in accord with neoclassical doctrine and decorum. His ode is to Evening, not to a specific evening.

6.2 William Wordsworth, 'The Solitary Reaper'

Our next poem is William Wordsworth's 'The Solitary Reaper':

> Behold her, single in the field,
> Yon solitary Highland Lass!
> Reaping and singing by herself;
> Stop here, or gently pass!
> Alone she cuts and binds the grain,
> And sings a melancholy strain;
> O listen! for the Vale profound
> Is overflowing with the sound.
>
> No Nightingale did ever chaunt
> More welcome notes to weary bands
> Of travellers in some shady haunt,
> Among Arabian sands:
> A voice so thrilling ne'er was heard
> In spring-time from the Cuckoo bird,
> Breaking the silence of the seas
> Among the farthest Hebrides.
>
> Will no one tell me what she sings?
> Perhaps the plaintive numbers flow
> For old, unhappy, far-off things,
> And battles long ago:
> Or is it some more humble lay,
> Familiar matter of today?
> Some natural sorrow, loss, or pain,
> That has been, and may be again?
>
> Whate'er the theme, the maiden sang
> As if her song could have no ending;

> I saw her singing at her work,
> And o'er the sickle bending;
> I listened till I had my fill:
> And as I mounted up the hill,
> The music in my heart I bore,
> Long after it was heard no more.

The first verse appears rather more excited than seems appropriate. Furnished with no less than three exclamation marks, it is almost as much about the observer as the woman he is looking at. 'Behold her . . . Stop here, or gently pass! . . . O listen!': there is an insistent, exclamatory buttonholing of an imaginary spectator (who might also be the reader), as though he or she might otherwise miss the significance of an apparently unremarkable scene. It is the woman's song which seems to entrance the poet, more than her appearance and certainly more than the work she is at. He tells us that the vale is 'overflowing with the sound' of her voice, which seems a bit hyperbolic. Is she really singing at full volume, or is this a perception stirred by something in the music which is more than the music? Anyway, the comment seems as excessive as the overflowing of the woman's voice, and we are in the dark as to why this might be so.

The next verse compares the woman's voice to the nightingale and the cuckoo, but in a structurally odd kind of way. What the poem says is that this human voice is far more soothing and thrilling than the chirping of these birds; but grammatically speaking it says it in such a way as to throw all the poetic emphasis upon the birds themselves – that is to say, on what is formally being dismissed as inferior. And this creates a certain disproportion in the verse, though one that it carries off without any notable strain. If you want to praise a woman's musical talent, you do not generally claim that her voice is more alluring than the sound of a cuckoo heard in springtime in the far-flung Hebrides where it seems to break the silence of the seas. Or that it is more welcome than the sound of a nightingale chanting to weary bands of travellers in a shady haunt in the sands of Arabia. By the time the eye arrives at the end of these clauses, the reader is in danger of forgetting that all this is something that the Highland lass's voice is superior to, and has begun to focus on the images as autonomous entities. Images which offer to illustrate end up by distracting.

This, in fact, is a quite common device in poetry. A version of it can be found in the line 'No star is o'er the lake, its pale watch keeping', where we are first told there is no star and then, contradictorily, that it is keeping its pale watch. What the line means is that there is no star, of the kind which customarily keeps its pale watch, over the lake; but the effect, as in the Wordsworth verse, is to dismiss the star and conjure it into presence at the same time. This also happens in T. S. Eliot's 'Gerontion':

> I was neither at the hot gates
> Nor fought in the warm rain
> Nor knee deep in the salt marsh, heaving a cutlass,
> Bitten by flies, fought.

All this is what the speaker *didn't* do. The gates he wasn't at were hot; the rain in which he didn't fight was warm; the salt marsh he didn't stand in came up to his knees; and the flies didn't bite him at the moment he wasn't swinging a cutlass.

The secret of this imbalance in Wordsworth's verse is probably that he is not particularly interested in the Highland lass herself. He is interested, rather, in the kind of thoughts and images she inspires in him, even if these images are formally offered as less precious than the woman herself. The fact that the third word of the piece is 'single' may be significant here: stark, solitary figures marooned in bleak landscapes are peculiarly evocative for Wordsworth, but they generally serve the purpose of pointing, like symbols, beyond themselves. It is the deeper imaginative dimension they evoke which really matters to him. The wanderers, small farmers and blind beggars who inspire him in this way rarely have much substance in themselves, and the same goes for the solitary reaper. It is her lonely self-absorption which seems to fascinate the speaker, who perhaps sees in it a reflection of his own poetic solitude. Not only a reflection, in fact, but an inspiration: her very enigmatic presence is a source of 'exotic' imagery for him. There may be a sense in which he is pointing excitedly to an image of himself. An idealised image, perhaps, since the woman seems to have a composure and autonomy about her which the poet himself might feel that he lacks. She does not seem to be anxious about being alone, and if she has spotted this poetically aroused English tourist lurking near her field she is clearly unperturbed by him.

It is the first line of the third verse which delivers the surprise punch: 'Will no one tell me what she sings?' Only now do we realise with a jolt that the speaker can't actually understand what the woman is singing about, presumably because she is singing in Scottish Gaelic. This, however, proves to be no great loss. On the contrary, it provides the poet with yet another flight of fancy, this time about what the lass *might* be singing about. The subjunctive mood trumps the indicative. Because he does not know the theme of her actual song, the speaker can treat it as a blank text on to which to project his own poetic fantasies. In fact, one suspects that query 'Will know one tell me what she sings?' is a purely rhetorical one – that he would really rather not know, since such determinacy of meaning would diminish the scope of his own musings. Because the song means nothing definite to him, it can mean more or less anything, or at least anything suitably melancholic. Wordsworth is in something like the situation of John Keats before the Grecian Urn, posing a series of breathless questions to it ('What men or gods are these? What maidens loath?') which are all the more gratifying because no very precise answers are available.

In the final verse, the speaker tells us that he listened to the woman until 'I had my fill'. He has reaped what gratification he wants from her, without even knowing who she is, and now he is ready to travel on. In a sense, then, it is he who is the solitary reaper. As he does pass on, he bears the music in his heart long after the woman herself is out of sight. But in a sense she was out of sight all along, as no more than a convenient figure around which to organise his own flights of fancy. He remembers the lass's music, but the experience seemed a kind of memory even when he was having it. He relates to her rather as a modern tourist relates to a medieval castle through a camera lens, content to know nothing of its history but assured of having garnered an image of it as a souvenir for the future.

So Wordsworth has had his momentous encounter with a symbolist poet – with a discourse in which he savours the signifier all the more keenly because the signified or meaning is obscure to him. One strength of the poem, as with much of Wordsworth's work, is that he does not seem to grasp exactly why the experience is so haunting and arresting, any more than he understands what the woman is singing. It is as though the impenetrability of her song, rather than its sweetness and certainly rather than the singer herself, touches in him a kind of obscurity too deep to articulate. One can see how this might be an alarming experience, as it can be elsewhere in Wordsworth: one stumbles upon an alien, solitary figure, absorbed in its own strange despondency, which seems to turn its back enigmatically on the poet himself. But the mood of the poem is not troubled or fearful, though it is part of its complex effect that we can glimpse how it might be.

Instead, the speaker draws a reflective pleasure from the sadness of the reaper's song; indeed, sadness in Wordsworth is often more consoling than distressing. Perhaps she is offering him a lesson in how to overcome sorrow by transforming it into art; so that his own poem, while partly on the subject of grief, is nevertheless tranquil and self-possessed. In this sense, the poem doubles what the reaper does. Whether this achievement is somehow bought at her expense is one of the questions the reader is left to ponder. The woman sings in a mournful way of what may well be tragic events (though they may well not be either); but it does not follow that she is downcast herself, and the fact that she carries on working while she is singing suggests that she isn't. The song is perhaps more a work ritual than personally expressive, so that it is gloomy but she is not. And this, too, might be something that Wordsworth learns from the experience. One can see how this might be a source of comfort to a poet given to fits of glumness. 'Melancholy' suggests a tempered kind of dejection, one which is far from distraught. Wordsworth might also draw a lesson from the fact that in certain circumstances, such as a labour chant, poetry can have a pragmatic value, which was scarcely obvious to most Romantic poets.

Rather than feeling threatened by the autonomy and anonymity of the reaper, the speaker seems anxious to preserve these qualities. This, perhaps, is the point of 'Stop here, or gently pass': he does not want to call attention to his presence because this would turn the woman from an observed object to a perceiving subject, thus ruining what is most evocative about her. In another version of the work, 'I listened till I had my fill' becomes the tautological 'I listened, motionless and still', like a man with a pair of binoculars who is trying not to scare off a rare but skittish bird. Anyhow, whatever it is which the experience touches in the poet, he is shrewd enough not to moralise it away. It is when Wordsworth tries to spell out the moral significance of these mute, cryptic, disorientating encounters that he is at his most tedious.

6.3 Gerard Manley Hopkins, 'God's Grandeur'

For our third Nature poem, we move to the other end of the nineteenth century and Gerard Manley Hopkins's 'God's Grandeur':

> The world is charged with the grandeur of God.
>   It will flame out, like shining from shook foil;
>   It gathers to a greatness, like the ooze of oil
> Crushed. Why do men then now not reck his rod?
> Generations have trod, have trod, have trod;
>   And all is seared with trade; bleared, smeared with toil;
>   And wears man's smudge and shares man's smell: the soil
> Is bare now, nor can foot feel, being shod.

> And for all this, nature is never spent;
>> There lives the dearest freshness deep down things;
>> And though the last lights off the black West went
>> Oh, morning, at the brown brink eastward, springs –
> Because the Holy Ghost over the bent
>> World broods with warm breast and with ah! bright wings.

There is an ambiguity running through this poem which does not instantly spring to the eye. Hopkins was a Roman Catholic priest, and Roman Catholics are officially free to believe either that Nature was involved in the Fall along with humanity, or that only humanity is fallen. This is more than just an academic issue, since if Nature is fallen then it cannot easily act as a medium of divine grace for human beings; whereas if it remains unfallen, it can provide post-lapsarian beings with just such a taste of innocence and joy.

'God's Grandeur' is perhaps most interestingly read as equivocating between these two positions. We are told to begin with, in an authoritative flourish, that 'The world is charged with the grandeur of God', and that this grace seems readily available: 'It will flame out like shining from shook foil'. But the foil in this finely wrought image has to be shaken in order to shine, which suggests that divine grace is not as readily available in Nature as all that. A certain effort (that of shaking the foil) is necessary to come by it. Nature is charged with grace, but it does not release it spontaneously. Hopkins, then, is able to avoid what for him would be two heretical extremes: on the one hand, the radical Protestant view that grace and Nature are absolutely at odds with one another, and on the other hand what is known as the Pelagian heresy, for which grace is natural to us. The poem needs to tread a fine line between denigrating Nature, which would be to forget that it is God's creation, and elevating it to divine status in a way which would run the risk of pantheism. The Catholic position here is that Nature, including human nature, has the potential for grace – it is, so to speak, predisposed to share in God's life – but that this sharing in the life of infinite love nevertheless requires a laborious self-transformation. Nature needs to go beyond itself to become truly itself; but it has the built-in capacity to do so, which radical Protestantism would deny. Grace is not spontaneous, but neither is it arbitrary. It does not already suffuse the world, but it is not alien to it either.

The same delicate tension is sustained in the next image: 'It gathers to a greatness, like the ooze of oil / Crushed'. 'Gathers to a greatness' suggests an organic, spontaneous process; but that 'Crushed' abruptly intervenes as we step across the line-ending to insist, once again, that human agency is involved here. The shift from one line to another is also a shift of perspective.

In a prefiguring of modern environmentalism, Hopkins then laments the way that Nature has been polluted by humanity. If the first lines of the poem emphasised the need for active human participation in the business of grace, we are now grimly reminded of how predatory such human activity can actually be. 'Generations have trod, have trod, have trod' is a touch too onomatopoeic, rather too obviously inviting us to hear the plodding of polluting feet in its sound and rhythm; but the packed sound-pattern of the next two lines, with their complex criss-crossing of assonance and alliteration, are richly expressive of human alienation from the natural world. The prejudice against shoes, though ('nor can foot feel, being shod'), is surely rather excessive. Is Hopkins really recommending a mass reversion to barefootedness?

The foot image, however, is in a sense consoling. It suggests that the problem is with us, not with Nature. Nature may still be as charged with grace as ever; it is just that we have insulated ourselves from it by our modern technologies. The same goes for words like 'smeared', 'bleared' and 'smudge', which suggests a purely surface contamination. Smearings, blearings and smudgings you can wipe off. '*Seared* with trade' is rather more troubling, since to sear is to scorch, and scorch marks cannot be rubbed off; but the general impression created by the imagery is of a Nature only superficially tainted by its most rapacious inhabitant. As the poem laments, then, its imagery simultaneously qualifies that lamentation. Nature cannot be seen as too deeply infected by humanity, since this might appear to question one's belief in its divine goodness, as well as to allot humanity itself too much cosmic significance. Surely men and women can't seriously despoil what God has created?

This sanguine view is then reinforced by the opening lines of the second stanza:

> And for all this, nature is never spent;
> There lives the dearest freshness deep down things . . .

('For' here means 'despite'.) Humanity may do its worst, but Nature's resources are inexhaustible. There is a play on words here with 'spent' and 'dearest', terms which have financial overtones. The commercialism which the poem has just been denouncing ('trade') now provides it unobtrusively with a source of imagery. Nature has the munificence of a benevolent billionaire, and will never go bankrupt. Yet in case we grow too complacent about its opulence, 'deep down' puts us on the alert. The freshness which lives in things is deep down, and thus, so the implication runs, not spontaneously available. We are back to shook foil and crushed oil. Hopkins must not play up the commonness of grace to the point where he plays down original sin. Perhaps it is just as well that Nature's treasures are so deeply stored, since then we are less able to defile them; but what keeps them secure is also what makes them hard to gain access to.

The poem's final, extraordinary image maintains this tension to the end:

> And though the last lights off the black West went
> Oh, morning, at the brown brink eastward, springs –
> Because the Holy Ghost over the bent
> World broods with warm breast and with ah! bright wings.

First we have the sanguine viewpoint again: Nature's freshness may seem to have vanished, but this is no more an irretrievable loss than the sun going down. The sun goes down (or, as the modern theory has it, the earth turns up) only to spring back up again in the morning. Grace would seem as universally available as light. Yet the last two lines of the poem implicitly rebuff this assumption. The coming and going of the light as the earth turns is itself the work of the Holy Spirit. It is because he sits like a brooding hen on the great egg of the globe that the light is hatched out of it each dawn. Daylight is not as natural and spontaneous as it seems. Like the shining of the foil and the gathering of the oil, it is the result of a labour. The world is 'bent', meaning both literally curved and morally corrupt; and only God's constant agency can conjure something beneficial from it. Hopkins has thus neatly avoided both pantheism, the doctrine which would see God and Nature as identical, and Pelagianism, a heresy which denies or denigrates the Fall of humanity. But he has done so while celebrating the dearness and freshness of the natural world, in a poignant contrast with human depravity.

Another way of looking at the poem is to see it as an allegory of poetry itself. Hopkins is renowned for the muscular inventiveness of his language, but we have seen already that this may well reflect a certain modernist suspicion of language, as well as a celebration of it. Language in its everyday state is, so to speak, fallen: it is bleared and smudged with trade, degraded to a mere instrument of commercial and bureaucratic communication; and to be stirred into life again, the poet must wreak what the Formalists, as we have seen, called a certain organised violence upon it. Hence all that Hopkinsian cramming and dislocating and burnishing of language, which some find gorgeous and others find merely eccentric. A hostile critic once remarked that Hopkins took the English language and left it a 'muscle-bound monstrosity'. Language in its common-or-garden state is no medium of grace and truth; but if you shake it and crush it, heightening, stretching and compressing its words, you may persuade it to release a precious insight. Poetry, like grace, does not come naturally. You have to work for them both. Yet poetry is not unnatural either. The creative imagination is a reflection of God's action within the individual; and like divine grace it 'redeems' the world by restoring it to us in all its pristine freshness.

There is a typically modernist 'extremism' behind this poetics. Truth is accessible only when you press things to their outer limit. Only in some Room 101 of the human spirit, faced with the vilest horror you can imagine, can you give voice to it. Everyday life, by contrast, is banal, illusory, inauthentic. You have to shake it very hard to get anything worthwhile out of it. The same goes for human beings, in a certain traditional conservative view of them. In their natural state men and women are indolent, selfish, violent creatures; only by disciplining and chastising them can you force anything half-decent out of them. Hopkins himself was a conservative, who found 'trade' distasteful from the standpoint of a spiritual aristocrat, not from that of a socialist. He was also something of an ascetic, concerned with subjugating the flesh. His poetics, like his politics, brood upon the way a stringent Jesuitical discipline (of rhythm, internal rhyme and so on) may bring the best out of its raw materials. If this is too gloomy a view of human nature, the opposing liberal vision tends to be too dewy-eyed. Human beings will do the right thing spontaneously if only you leave them to their own devices. It is pushing them around which causes all the trouble.

6.4   Edward Thomas, 'Fifty Faggots'

The final work to examine is Edward Thomas's 'Fifty Faggots', written early in the twentieth century:

> There they stand, on their ends, the fifty faggots
> That once were underwood of hazel and ash
> In Jenny Pinks's Copse. Now, by the hedge
> Close packed, they make a thicket fancy alone
> Can creep through with the mouse and wren. Next Spring
> A blackbird or a robin will nest there,
> Accustomed to them, thinking they will remain
> Whatever is for ever to a bird.
> This Spring it is too late; the swift has come,
> 'Twas a hot day for carrying them up:
> Better they will never warm me, though they must
> Light several Winters' fires. Before they are done

The war will have ended, many other things
Have ended, maybe, that I can no more
Foresee or more control than robin and wren.

It is a change to find a poet actually working in the midst of Nature. In Collins's 'Ode to Evening' we see no signs of labour at all, and the poet's stance to the landscape is purely contemplative. (Much the same is true of the novels of Jane Austen, which hardly ever portray anybody at work on the landed estates which form their backdrop.) Wordsworth is watching someone else working but not working himself, and the reaper's labour is not the focus of his attention. The Hopkins poem is sharply critical of work upon the natural world, which it can see only as a form of ravage and pollution. In this poem, however, Nature is not a landscape to be surveyed but a working environment to be engaged with. Work is the process by which human beings transform their natural environment in order to meet their needs, and Thomas makes no sentimental apology for hacking faggots (or bundles of firewood) from a copse. Country people need to keep warm in winter, and relate to Nature not primarily as an aesthetic object but in terms of its use-value.

It is generally town-dwellers who gaze upon Nature as a timeless aesthetic spectacle, in what one might call the day-tripper view of the countryside. They do not typically see Nature as fuel and food – as something to eat as well as something to stare at. Whereas 'Fifty Faggots' is clearly a poem by someone who lives in a rural environment, knows his way around and names the landscape in familiar local terms ('Jenny Pinks's Copse') rather than, like Collins, in the more exalted nomenclature of myth and allegory. Nature comes to us not 'in itself', but as socially mediated: Thomas is interested in the way it is woven through with human meanings and purposes, and not just human ones either: even the birds see Nature not as a reality in itself but as somewhere to nest.

Even so, this is not a natural landscape which is *centred* on the human. 'Man' is not lord of all he surveys, appropriating what he wants from Nature with the consumerist lack of effort of a Wordsworth plucking memories like pansies as he wanders on his way. Thomas's relationship to Nature is among other things one of sweat and struggle: carrying the faggots up to the hedge was an arduous business, which he tells us with a pleasant touch of wit has warmed him more than the fires that the wood is intended for ever will. Nature is not a blank text to be inscribed as the fancy takes you, but recalcitrant stuff with a life of its own.

The closing lines of the piece – '. . . many other things / Have ended, maybe, that I can no more / Foresee or more control than robin and wren'

indeterminacy: lack of clear or exact meaning.

inscape: a term coined by Gerard Manley Hopkins to denote the essence or typical inner form of a phenomenon.

metaphor: the use of language which is imaginatively but not literally appropriate (e.g. 'nobody, not even the rain, has such small hands'), or the representation of a thing by another thing which resembles it.

metonymy: the representation of a thing by another thing which is part of or associated with it, e.g. 'crown' for 'monarchy' or 'turf' for horseracing.

metre: a regular kind of poetic sound pattern, one generally determined by the length of a line and stresses of the feet (or groups of syllables) which compose it.

metrical foot: a group of stressed and unstressed syllables which forms the basic unit of a line of poetry, e.g. an iamb (*di-dum*) or a trochee (*dum-di*).

mimetic: imitative.

mimetic fallacy: the belief that, say, a poem about boredom should itself be boring.

mock-heroic: a literary work which uses heroic forms and images in a debunking, satirical way.

mood: the emotional climate or ambience of a piece of writing.

paradigmatic: in semiotic theory, the relations between units of a literary text and the totality they constitute, rather than their relations with their immediate neighbours.

para-rhyme: a near-miss of a rhyme; two words (e.g. 'bliss' and 'bless') which sound alike but do not rhyme exactly. More exactly, a semi-rhyme in which the consonantal sounds agree but the vowels do not.

parataxis: the juxtaposition of clauses without indicating the connections between them.

pathetic fallacy: the assigning of human feelings to natural objects.

performative: concerning language as an action or event, rather than simply as a structure of meanings.

phatic: language relating to the act of communication itself, e.g. 'Good to talk to you!'

phonic: relating to sound.

poetics: the study or theory of poetry.

pragmatic: concerning practical uses and consequences.

rhythm: the variable pattern of accented and unaccented syllables in an utterance, as opposed to the invariant pattern of metre.

semantic: relating to meaning.

semiotics: the study of signs.

signified: a concept or meaning.

signifier: a sound or written mark which denotes a concept or meaning.

simile: figure of speech comparing one thing with another.

sonnet: a poem of fourteen lines, usually iambic pentameters, the classical form of which divides into two sections: an eight-line octave and a six-line sestet.

stanza: a verse of a poem, composed in a particular metrical and rhyming form which is then repeated in the other verses.

structure: a phenomenon (such as a poem) considered as a set of organised, interconnected parts.

synecdoche: the use of a part of a whole to indicate the whole, e.g. 'There were three new faces at the meeting.'

syntagmatic: in semiotic theory, the relations of a literary unit with what immediately precedes and follows it, as in a syntactical chain.

syntax: the organisation of phrases and clauses into sentences.

tetrameter: a line of four feet (or metrical units).

texture: the pattern of sounds of a poem.

timbre: the distinctive quality of a voice, used metaphorically of the unique character of a poet's linguistic style.

tone: the sound, pitch, pace and intensity of a poem considered as expressing a particular emotion.

trimeter: a line of three feet.

trochee: a metrical unit with one stressed and one unstressed syllable (*dum-di*).

trope: figurative use of language.

Index

Printed and bound by CPI Group (UK) Ltd, Croydon, CR0 4YY
13/07/2021
03076210-0001